W9-AUY-199

NATIVE SON
The Story of Richard Wright

NATIVE SON
The Story of Richard Wright

Joyce Hart

Central Rappahannock Regional Library
1201 Caroline Street
Fredericksburg, VA 22401

MORGAN REYNOLDS
Publishing, Inc.

620 South Elm Street, Suite 223
Greensboro, North Carolina 27406
http://www.morganreynolds.com

YA
921
Wrigh
C.2

NATIVE SON: THE STORY OF RICHARD WRIGHT

Copyright © 2003 by Joyce Hart

All rights reserved.
This book, or parts thereof, may not be reproduced in any form except
by written consent of the publisher. For information write:
Morgan Reynolds, Inc., 620 S. Elm St., Suite 223
Greensboro, North Carolina 27406 USA

Library of Congress Cataloging-in-Publication Data

Hart, Joyce.
  Native son : the story of Richard Wright / Joyce Hart.-- 1st ed.
    p. cm. -- (World writers)
Summary: Traces the life and achievements of the twentieth-century African American
novelist, whose early life was shaped by a strict grandmother who had been a slave, an
illiterate father, and a mother educated as a schoolteacher.
  Includes bibliographical references and index.
  Contents: A troubling beginning -- Facing Jim Crow laws -- Finding a voice -- Exploring
the Communist Party -- First book -- Reaching the masses -- Breaking ties -- Writing his
autobiography -- Returning to poetry.
  ISBN 1-931798-06-0 (lib. bdg.)
  1. Wright, Richard, 1908-1960--Juvenile literature. 2. Authors, American--20th
century--Biography--Juvenile literature. 3. African American authors--Biography--Juvenile
literature. [1. Wright, Richard, 1908-1960. 2. Authors, American. 3. African
Americans--Biography.] I. Title. II. Series.

PS3545.R815 Z668 2002
813'.52--dc21

                                              2002013686

Printed in the United States of America
First Edition

World Writers

Gwendolyn Brooks

Richard Wright

Henry Wadsworth Longfellow

Nathaniel Hawthorne

Stephen Crane

F. Scott Fitzgerald

Langston Hughes

Washington Irving

Edgar Rice Burroughs

H.G. Wells

Sir Arthur Conan Doyle

Isaac Asimov

Bram Stoker

Mary Shelley

Ida Tarbell

George Orwell

Mary Wollstonecraft

Elizabeth Cary

Marguerite Henry

To my children

Contents

Richard Wright. *(Courtesy of the Yale Collection of American Literature, Beinecke Rare Book and Manuscript Library.)*

Chapter One

A Troubling Beginning

When he was four years old, Richard Wright set his grandparents' house on fire. His mother had left him and his little brother alone in the living room. She was busy tending to his sick grandmother in bed upstairs and told him to watch his brother and warned him to keep quiet and stay still.

Richard was soon bored. The only interesting thing in the room was the fire in the fireplace. He pulled a few straws from a broom and tossed them into the fire. The straws flared and died down. He tried putting even more straws in the fire, but they were quickly consumed. Looking for something that would burn longer, he tugged the curtains and held them over the fire until they burst into flames. The little house filled with smoke.

Richard knew he was in big trouble. He ran outside and crawled under the burning house. His parents ran into the yard, searching frantically for him. Half the house above Richard was engulfed in flames. His mother screamed out his name while his father scurried about looking for him. Finally, his father looked under the porch, saw Richard, crawled under the burning house, and pulled him out by his feet.

Richard survived the blaze, and his mother's beating, but the incident did not squelch his tendency to rebel. Throughout his life, he felt that trouble was his constant companion. Whether he was living in his grandmother's home in Mississippi as a youth, or walking down the crowded streets of New York City as an adult, trouble always seemed to be waiting around the next corner for Richard Wright.

Richard was born on September 4, 1908, in Roxie, Mississippi, a time and place in which trouble was a daily part of the lives of many African Americans. Richard's grandfather, Nathaniel Wright, and his grandmother, Margaret Bolton Wilson, also known as Maggie, were freed slaves. They told Richard stories about the hardships they had endured and witnessed. The stories sparked Richard's curiosity and created in him a budding sense of angry rebellion. Why had such cruelties been allowed to happen? Why had his grandparents done nothing to stop it? Richard seldom received satisfactory answers from them. They were afraid to blame anyone for the cruelties they had suffered, fearing that if they did, they might once again be punished. Richard was told to not ask such questions. He should learn to accept life as it had been handed to him.

The experience of slavery had particularly embit-

100 DOLLARS
REWARD!

Ranaway from the subscriber on the 27th of July, my Black Woman, named

EMILY,

Seventeen years of age, well grown, black color, has a whining voice. She took with her one dark calico and one blue and white dress, a red corded gingham bonnet; a white striped shawl and slippers. I will pay the above reward if taken near the Ohio river on the Kentucky side, or THREE HUNDRED DOLLARS, if taken in the State of Ohio, and delivered to me near Lewisburg, Mason County, Ky.   THO'S. H. WILLIAMS.
August 4, 1853.

Richard's grandparents were born into slavery, and the stories they shared about their experiences made their grandson scared and angry. This nineteenth century document advertises a reward for the capture of a runaway slave. Slavery was officially abolished in the United States after the passage of the Thirteenth Amendment in 1865. *(Courtesy of the Library of Congress.)*

tered Richard's grandmother. She seldom laughed or showed any emotion other than anger. She did not understand Richard's natural curiosity and his inability to conform to the way of life that she dictated. Richard was a constant distraction for his grandmother Maggie, just as she was a continuous restraint on Richard's life.

Richard's father, Nathan, worked on a farm. Nathan never learned to read. He did not understand the importance of books and gaining knowledge about the world, aside from knowing how to grow crops and make enough money to put food on the table.

Richard's mother, Ella, on the other hand, had received enough education to teach school. Ella's parents had not been in favor of her marrying Nathan, but Ella had insisted. Unfortunately, Ella had to give up her job

Richard Wright's grandmother Maggie Wilson was a freed slave. *(Courtesy of the Yale Collection of American Literature, Beinecke Rare Book and Manuscript Library.)*

Richard's mother, Ella, taught school before marrying Nathan Wright. *(Courtesy of the Yale Collection of American Literature, Beinecke Rare Book and Manuscript Library.)*

as a teacher in order to help Richard's father work on the farm. She also washed clothes and cleaned other people's houses to earn extra money, leaving her with little time to spend with Richard.

Despite the fact that Richard spent his early childhood on a farm, he seldom had enough to eat. The main crop that was grown in the fields surrounding his house was cotton. Roxie, Mississippi was one of the poorest places to live in the United States at the time that Richard was growing up.

Going hungry was something that Richard knew well. As he got older, the hunger increased because the money his family made became more and more scarce. "Hunger had always been more or less at my elbow when I played," Richard wrote. "But now I began to wake up at night to find hunger standing at my bedside . . . This new hunger baffled me, scared me, made me angry and insistent."

In 1911, when Richard was three years old, his family moved to Memphis, Tennessee, so that his father could search for a better-paying job. The metropolitan city of Memphis was much different than rural Mississippi. Nathan found a job working as a night porter in a Beale Street drugstore. Ella, Nathan, and the two boys shared one bedroom and a kitchen in a tenement house.

Richard's father, Nathan Wright, abandoned his family when his oldest son was five years old. *(Courtesy of the Yale Collection of American Literature, Beinecke Rare Book and Manuscript Library.)*

Nathan worked at night and slept during the day. Richard and his one-year-old brother, Leon, were told to remain quiet while their father slept.

One day while Nathan was trying to sleep, he became annoyed by the sounds of a hungry kitten in the backyard. He told Richard to get rid of the cat, but the kitten refused to leave and continued to cry. Nathan yelled out of the window: "Kill that damn thing!"

Richard, knowing that Nathan had not really meant what he said, decided to outsmart him. If Richard were only doing as he was told, how could his father punish him if he really did kill the cat? He found a rope and hanged the kitten.

When Ella discovered what Richard had done, she punished him severely. "You owe a debt you can never pay," she told him. In the darkness of late evening, she made Richard bury the kitten and pray for forgiveness.

Not long after this incident, Richard's father abandoned his family, leaving them without money or food. The family struggled until Richard's mother found a job as a cook. She made enough money to pay the rent and buy food, but she could not afford to have someone watch her children. Richard and his younger brother stayed home alone when Ella went to work.

Richard, only six years old, freely roamed the neighborhood while his mother was away at work. One day he stood peering underneath the swinging doors of a saloon when a man caught him by the arm and pulled him inside. The sounds and smells of the saloon scared him. "The odor of alcohol stung my nostrils. I yelled and struggled, trying to break free of him, afraid of the staring crowd of men and women, but he would not let me go." The man sat Richard up on the bar and put his hat on Richard's head. The people in the bar said Richard was cute and thought it would be funny to hear him use foul language. They gave him money to repeat what they whispered in his ear. They also paid Richard to drink alcohol. For pennies and nickels, young Richard wandered back to the bar day after day. He often came home in a drunken daze. Ella finally realized what had been happening and immediately found a woman to look after her sons and keep them off the streets.

When Ella was home, she often read to Richard and told him stories. She helped him sound out words in the Sunday paper. One day while Ella was at work, a delivery man taught Richard how to count to one hundred. Ella stood speechless as her young son counted as high as he could.

Richard started school at the Howe Institute in Memphis in 1915. He had just turned seven and was terrified of going to school. His time there was cut short, however, when Ella became sick and Richard had to stay home and care for her. Richard's grandmother, Maggie Wilson, came to stay with the family and take care of Ella. Maggie's brief stay provided some financial respite for Ella and the boys, but as soon as she left Memphis, the money she had brought was gone as well.

Without enough money to buy food for her children, Ella placed Richard and his brother in the Settlement House, an orphanage for young children. The orphan-

The NAACP hung this banner from the window of its headquarters in New York City to announce the mob killing of a black man in 1936. According to the NAACP, for the thirty year period between 1889 to 1919, over three thousand lynchings took place in the United States. *(Courtesy of the Library of Congress.)*

age did little to satisfy Richard's hunger. He and the other children were constantly hungry. Just as he was afraid on his first day of school, Richard was also scared at the Settlement House. He worried that his mother had abandoned him and his brother. They stayed there just over a month, until Ella's sister, also named Maggie, invited them to live with her in Arkansas.

Maggie and her husband, Silas Hoskins, owned a saloon that catered to African Americans. He and Maggie lived quite comfortably off of the money they earned from the saloon. Richard enjoyed staying with his Aunt Maggie, who often stood up for him when his mother scolded him. He especially enjoyed the meals Aunt Maggie served. Richard was not accustomed to having food and often slipped biscuits into his pocket to save for later.

Richard had not been in Arkansas long when a young black man knocked on Aunt Maggie's door to inform her that Silas had been killed by a group of white men who were jealous of the money he made from the saloon. Maggie, Ella, Richard, and Leon fled town, afraid they might be killed next.

Richard's life continued to deteriorate. By the time he was eleven, his family had moved from city to city looking for work. He was never able to stay in one school for long. Due to his mother's failing health, he was often required to drop out of school and work odd jobs, such as delivering groceries. Then in 1920, his mother suffered a devastating stroke that left her partially paralyzed. Ella and her sons had to move back to Mississippi and live there with her parents in Jackson.

In September 1921, Richard entered the fifth grade at the Jim Hill Primary School just up the street from his grandmother's house in Jackson. Most of the students at Jim Hill were of the black middle class. At thirteen, Richard was two years older than his fellow schoolmates, but he worked hard and quickly advanced to the sixth grade. The students at Jim Hill studied hard and took an interest in academics. Surrounded by studious classmates, Richard discovered his love of reading. The power of words amazed him. Unfortunately, Richard's religious grandmother, Maggie, believed that any book not approved by her church was information straight from the devil. A former schoolteacher, Ella supported

Richard, (back row, fifth from left) was selected as valedictorian of his high school class. *(Courtesy of the Yale Collection of American Literature, Beinecke Rare Book and Manuscript Library.)*

her son's love of literature, but she was debilitated by her illness and could do little to help him. He had to sneak books into the house.

Although Richard had moved from a poor life in Memphis, his grandmother Maggie's household in Jackson offered little financial relief. Maggie did not allow him to work on Saturdays, the Sabbath, or the holiest day of the week according to her religion, the Seventh-day Adventist church. There were few good jobs available for a black boy that did not require working on Saturdays, and Richard had trouble earning enough money to buy his textbooks. He wore clothes that had been patched many times. His friends worked after school and all day Saturday and had enough money to buy clothes, textbooks, and hearty lunches on schooldays. When they asked Richard to go to lunch with them, he would lie and tell them that he had already eaten.

Despite his constant hunger, shabby clothes, and lack of textbooks, Richard was determined to learn. In 1924, he entered the eighth grade at Smith Robertson Junior High School on the other side of Jackson. His teachers liked him and let him watch over the class if they needed to step out. They knew Richard was a serious student, and they thought highly of him.

Richard tried his hand at writing in class. One day he took out his composition book and decided to write a story. Although he had little training as a writer, he had read enough to know how to come up with a plot, or storyline. He wanted to write about a "villain who wanted a widow's home." He called it "The Voodoo of Hell's Half-Acre." He wrote the story in three days. When it was finished, he took it to the local black newspaper, the *Southern Register*, and was surprised when the editor decided to publish it. Richard began thinking he might want to become a writer.

In May 1925, Richard graduated at the top of his class at Smith Robertson Junior High School. He was chosen class valedictorian and would deliver a speech at graduation. He wrote a speech for the ceremony, but the principal, Professor Lanier, gave him a new one to read instead. Lanier knew that white people would attend the graduation ceremony, and he did not want

Richard to say anything to offend them. "I know what's best for you. You can't afford to just say *anything* before those white people that night," Lanier told Richard. "The superintendent of schools will be there; you're in a position to make a good impression on him . . . I've seen many a boy and girl graduate from this school, and none of them was too proud to recite a speech I wrote for them." Richard could feel his anger rising. He already had his own speech and was determined to give it. He told Lanier that "the people are coming to hear the students, and I won't make a speech that you've written."

The principal threatened Richard that he would not graduate, despite the fact that he had passed all his exams. Next he tried to bribe Richard by promising to help him get a job. Richard stood firm. "You're just a young, hot fool," Lanier said coolly. Richard was hurt by Lanier's comments, but he did not change his mind.

Richard titled his speech, "The Attributes of Life." Although he admitted that Lanier's speech sounded clearer than his, it did not say what Richard wanted to say. When he finished speaking, Richard heard a slight applause from some of his friends, but he did not wait around to hear any more about it. "I did not care if they liked it or not; I was through . . . and tried to shun all memory of the event from me." That speech marked the end of his formal education.

Richard had broken so many of his grandmother's rules by the time he graduated from ninth grade that she ignored him completely. His mother was ill and relied on Richard's grandmother for food and shelter. Ella was the only family member who embraced Richard, but she was unable to give him the support he would need to finish his high school studies. It was 1925, and Richard was seventeen. As he explained it, it was time that he "faced the world."

Chapter Two

Memphis

Richard was anxious to live on his own but needed to get a job and save money before he could leave his grandmother's house. Although Richard had excelled in his educational career, he did not learn many skills about working in the white world of Jackson. He did not understand that black people were expected to act un-intelligent and obedient towards their white bosses. Black workers often went underpaid, and many of Richard's friends tried to convince him that stealing from their white bosses was the only way they could get more money. Richard did not agree.

Richard took a job working as a porter in Farley's clothing store. The store sold clothing on credit to black people. White people ran the store, and Richard always remembered how they treated their black customers. "The shop was always crowded with black men and women pawing over cheap suits and dresses. And they paid whatever price the white man asked. The boss, his son, and the clerk treated the Negroes with open contempt, pushing, kicking, or slapping them. No matter how often I witnessed it, I could not get used to it."

One day Richard stood outside polishing the brass doorknob when his boss and boss's son drove up in front of the store. The two men stepped out and pulled a black woman from the back seat, then dragged her into the store. Richard recalled that, "After a moment or two I heard shrill screams coming from the rear room of the store; later the woman stumbled out, bleeding, crying, holding her stomach, her clothing torn." A nearby white policeman arrested the woman for being drunk. Later, Richard went to the back of the store and saw blood on the floor. "Boy, that's what we do to niggers when they don't pay their bills," Richard's boss told him. Richard had never seen his boss treat white customers in this way. He had never seen a policeman accuse a white woman, who was bleeding from wounds on her body, of being drunk. He questioned these actions but knew better than to ask his boss for answers.

A couple of days later, Richard's boss told him to take the bike from the back of the store and deliver some packages to a house across town. Richard was riding through a white neighborhood when one of the bicycle tires went flat. As he walked the bike along the road, a car full of white men slowed by his side. One of the men asked Richard if he needed a ride, and Richard accepted the offer. He hopped onto the running board of the car and held tightly to his bicycle. Once he was securely set, the car sped ahead.

As the men drove along, they shared a bottle of whiskey. Richard watched as they passed the flask back and forth. One of them asked Richard if he wanted a drink. "Oh, no!" Richard replied. Richard had hardly spoken before he felt a hard object pelt him between the eyes. The men had flung the empty bottle out of the window at him. He let go of the door and fell from the moving vehicle. One of his legs became entangled in the spokes of his bike. The car stopped a few feet ahead and the men walked back to where Richard lay. His knees and elbows bled as he stood in a daze looking at the men. "Ain't you learned to say *sir* to a white man yet?" one of the men shouted at Richard. The man raised his fists and wanted to fight Richard, but one of the other passengers warned him not too. They told Richard that he was lucky they had decided not to kill him. Soon after the incident, he was fired for reading during his lunch break.

Although Richard's life had been spared in the bicycle incident, untold numbers of African Americans were killed in the early part of the twentieth century. No one was usually charged with the murders. An estimated five thousand African Americans were lynched, or brutally murdered, between the 1890s and the 1960s in the United States. These victims usually received no trial, and crowds of people gathered to watch them be beaten.

When Richard was still a teenager, the vast majority of African Americans still lived in the South under a system of strict legal segregation. The laws were made .

possible by a willful misinterpretation of a decision made by the U.S. Supreme Court. On June 7, 1892, an African-American man name Homer Plessy went to jail in Louisiana because he sat in a railroad car that was designated for whites. Plessy believed he had every right to sit in any seat on the train, and he refused to move to the seats that were marked for "colored" people. Plessy went to court and argued that the Separate Car Act, which designated separate train cars for black people, was illegal. John Howard Ferguson, the judge who heard Plessy's case, ruled against him. In 1896, the Supreme Court heard Plessy's case and upheld Judge Ferguson's decision. White officials in the South interpreted this decision to mean that they could deny black people equal social, educational, and economic opportunities. They emphasized the court's use of the word "separate," ignored the word "equal," and began to pass the so-called Jim Crow laws. The term "Jim Crow," which became a nickname for the segregation laws that the South practiced, was taken from the lyrics of a song sung by white male actors who blackened their faces and performed in minstrel shows that were popular in the late 1800s.

The South observed the "separate" portion of the decision with everything from separate water fountains to separate schools for black and white people. Schools for white children received sufficient funding, but schools for black children often had no desks or textbooks. The Ku Klux Klan, a white supremacist group, often preached that African Americans belonged to a

Under segregation, public places such as restaurants and bus stations could force black people to use separate facilities from whites. This North Carolina cafe had separate entrances for blacks and whites. *(Courtesy of the Library of Congress.)*

degenerate, diseased race that would totally be wiped out in a few generations. They began to dispense acts of cruelty against blacks, dismissing African Americans as less than human.

African-American children such as Richard heard stories about lynchings and other forms of torture. Many of them grew up afraid to confront white people in any way that might offend them. Black children learned not to look white people in the eye. They also knew not to speak in a tone of voice that showed offence or pride.

Richard never understood why black people acted so strangely around white people. Sometimes he guessed the correct procedure to follow, but just as often he guessed wrong. Many times he misjudged situations involving white people.

Richard tried hard to be humble, but it was difficult. It meant that he had to accept white people's definitions of who he was, that his very existence ranked somewhere beneath them and that he was inferior. He was threatened when he went against the conventional ways of the South, but he would not stop believing in himself. He knew he was smarter than many of the white people who wanted to control him. He paid close attention to their world, searching for a way to escape their power and realize his dreams.

Richard took a number of different jobs his first years out of school. At work he often overheard people talking about how different life was in the North. Many black people moved to northern cities to find better paying jobs and a better life. The North was not without its own racial problems, but many African Americans considered it a place of hope. Richard began to dream of going there.

Richard was determined to move north. He almost starved himself trying to save money. In less than a year after his graduation, Richard had worked enough odd jobs and saved enough money to buy a train ticket from Jackson, Mississippi to Memphis, Tennessee. Memphis was not exactly the North, but it was one step closer. Before leaving Mississippi, Richard promised his mother he would send for her as soon as he had earned enough money to rent a nice apartment.

Memphis, although still a southern town, was not as confining as Jackson. Richard remembered the town from the time he spent there as a young child, although it had grown immensely since then. He quickly found a room to live in and a job that offered better pay than he had earned before. He soon learned, however, that he had not escaped racial prejudice. He had both good and bad experiences in Tennessee. One of the worst experiences threatened his life. One of the better ones pushed him closer to his dream of becoming a writer.

Richard had two jobs in Memphis. He worked as both a dishwasher at a restaurant and a delivery boy for the Merry Optical Company. One day at the optical company, Richard's boss, Mr. Olin, began talking to him as if he were concerned about Richard. Mr. Olin, a white man, told Richard that a young African-American man named Harrison had been looking for him. He said that Harrison, who worked across the street at a rival optical company, had a grudge against Richard, and he had better keep his eye on him. After making Richard nervous, Mr. Olin patted him on the shoulder, saying he hoped there would be no bloodshed between the two youths. Richard was confused. He had never done or said anything to offend Harrison. He hardly knew the young man, but on the other hand, he could not understand why his boss would make up such a story. At lunchtime, Richard went across the street to where Harrison worked and confronted him.

In the course of their conversation, the young men realized that they had both been set up. "We two black boys, each working for ten dollars a week, stood staring at each other, thinking, comparing the motives of the absent white man, each asking himself if he could believe the other," Richard said. "He's trying to make us kill each other for nothing," he told Harrison. The next day, Mr. Olin said that Harrison was carrying a knife and asked if Richard owned one. Although Harrison did not scare Richard, Mr. Olin said that he was a fool not to protect himself. When Mr. Olin set a knife down on the table, Richard took it, afraid he might get fired if he refused. "Now, you're acting like a nigger with some sense," his boss told him.

For the next few weeks, the men at the optical company continued to egg Richard on to fight Harrison. The men realized that he was intent on avoiding a knife fight and offered to pay Richard and Harrison five dollars each if they would box. Richard did not want to fight, even with gloves on. He especially did not want to fight for the pleasure of white men. However, Harrison wanted the money and eventually talked him into the match. The boys promised to throw fake punches for four rounds, then take the money and run. Once they stepped into the ring, however, things changed.

Neither boy knew how to box, and their first swings were wild and unstructured. The white men jeered and called for blood. Richard felt humiliated and wanted to leave as soon as possible, but his next swing turned out to be too hard and busted Harrison's lip. Harrison got angry and struck back. As Richard described it, "Our plans and promises now meant nothing. We fought four hard rounds, stabbing, slugging, grunting, spitting, cursing, crying, bleeding." In the end, the men paid each boy, and Richard and Harrison never spoke to one another again.

Not all white men in Memphis acted cruelly towards Richard. Mr. Falk, a man Richard knew from the optical company, allowed Richard to use his library card, something black people were not allowed to have. In order to use the card, Richard pretended that he was picking up library books for Mr. Falk. Richard had often gone with notes to the library to pick up books for other people and knew the procedure. This time, Richard forged a note from Mr. Falk to the librarian: "*Dear madam: Will you please let this nigger boy . . . have some books by H. L. Mencken?*" He hoped that by using the derogatory term "nigger," the librarian would not suspect that he had written the note for himself. However, he was a little more nervous than usual when he took his own note to the library and waited for the librarian to read it.

Richard's plan almost backfired on him. The librarian questioned Richard about where he had gotten the library card and the note. "You're not using these books, are you?" she asked. Richard lied and said no. Despite the librarian's suspicions, Richard's plan worked. He went back and told Mr. Falk about the book he had checked out from the library. Mr. Falk enjoyed seeing Richard take an interest in literature. He and Richard often spoke about what they read.

Richard had never read good literature before, only second-hand schoolbooks and magazines. He wondered how anyone could write such clear and profound sentences. He read H.L. Menken's *Prejudices*, a book that criticized the Jim Crow laws. Richard had read about Mencken in a newspaper editorial criticizing the author of *Prejudices*. The editor of newspaper despised Mencken's criticisms of the racist South.

The more Richard read Mencken, the more he realized that words could be used as weapons. "Yes, this man [Mencken] was fighting, fighting with words," Richard realized. Richard wanted to use words in the same way. He began to understand the power of writing. What surprised Richard the most were not Mencken's words, "but how on earth anybody had the courage to say it." He read other great writers such as Joseph Conrad, Sinclair Lewis, Fyodor Dostoevski, Maxim Gorky, Theodore Dreiser, and others who would leave a lasting impression on him.

Although Richard loved to read, he had very little

time in the day. He began staying up all night. The stories he read illustrated everything that happened during his time. He began to understand the people around him better because he read stories about people who were just like them. The books were giving him glimpses into lives that he never imagined. He tried to write his own stories but his attempts came out flat. He realized that it would take more than desire to create good stories.

As Richard became a more avid reader, the walls of the South started closing in on him again. He had to find a way to move further North—the only place that held promise. To be a writer, he had to break free of the oppression of Southern culture. Richard's mother and brother had moved to Memphis to be with him. Now Richard began planning to take his family to Chicago.

Chapter Three

Finding a Voice

Richard was not a gambling man, but he feared that if he did not take a big chance and leave immediately for Chicago, he would be stuck in the South forever. Richard and his Aunt Maggie, who had been living with his family in Memphis, decided to move to Chicago. They planned to stay with Richard's Aunt Cleo until they found jobs and a place to live, then they would send for the others. Richard's mom was still ill, and his brother had trouble keeping a job. Maggie and Richard were the ones most able to go. "Finally sheer wish and hope prevailed over common sense and facts," Richard wrote.

Richard's mom and brother returned to Mississippi as Richard and his Aunt Maggie set out for Chicago. When he reached the city, Richard felt that for the first time in his life he had entered a world without racial barriers. He saw no doorways or facilities with signs reading "For Colored People" or "For White People."

He immediately noticed that white people and black people mingled together on the streets. This fascinated Richard, but his doubts and fears about how to survive in this new way of life kept him alert.

He and Aunt Maggie caught a bus, and Maggie pointed toward an empty seat, motioning for Richard to sit down. He obeyed but felt awkward sitting next to a white man. He made sure to look straight ahead, afraid to look at the man. Richard stole glances at the man and noticed that he was looking out of the window. The man appeared to take no notice of Richard at all.

Maggie and Richard stepped off the bus at the address that Aunt Cleo had given them. Her apartment turned out to be one room in a tenement house in the South Side of Chicago. The three of them could not live there together. Richard and Maggie rented a room across the hall. Richard was determined to find a job so that he would be able to pay for a larger apartment for his mother and brother.

Richard went out the next morning, and a cold wind took away his breath. It was the middle of December 1927, and the temperature barely reached above zero. Richard had never experienced winter in the North, and his threadbare clothing offered no protection from the bitter weather. He pushed himself forward in the stiff gale, holding onto his coat and lowering his head to keep the wind out of his eyes. After walking a few blocks, he saw a sign in the window of a delicatessen and walked in to apply for the job of porter.

The woman inside acted friendly towards Richard,

and he grew suspicious. He was not accustomed to white people speaking sincerely to a black person. She told Richard that he would have to wait for her husband, Mr. Hoffman, in order to apply for the position. She suggested that Richard wait inside the warm store until her husband returned. Richard felt very uncomfortable with Mrs. Hoffman's offer. He did not understand her generosity and turned down her offer. He struggled to keep warm outside the store, where he waited thirty minutes in the freezing temperatures.

Richard's life in the South had been very difficult, but he understood the unwritten social codes of conduct there. In Chicago he felt as though he had to learn a whole new language. How was he supposed to respond to Mrs. Hoffman's offer? What was the right thing to do? He was freezing in the cold air, but Richard waited nonetheless. He finally met with Mr. Hoffman, who told him the job was his if he wanted it.

Within a few days, Richard grew to like the Hoffmans. He still could not trust that they liked him, although they gave every sign that they appreciated all the work he did. After working for the Hoffmans for several weeks, Richard heard about a job with the U.S. Post Office that offered a better salary. He would have to pass a written examination, which he was confident that he could do.

Richard worried about taking time off from his job with the Hoffmans. Instead of asking for the day off to take the exam, he did not show up for work. The next day, Mr. Hoffman asked Richard where he had been.

Richard could not tell him the truth. In the South, if he told his boss that he had taken the exam, he might have been ridiculed or beaten, but he most certainly would have been fired. Richard stammered in response to Mr. Hoffman's question and then blurted out that his mother had died and he had to make an emergency trip back to Memphis. Mr. Hoffman knew that Richard was lying, but he forgave him. Richard felt ashamed: "Working with them from day to day and knowing that they knew I had lied from fear crushed me. I knew that they pitied me and pitied the fear in me." At the end of the week, Richard collected his pay and quit his job.

Richard bounced from one job to another. Each new job gave him a sense of progress, from salary increases to learning new skills. He worked for a short time as a busboy at a small café. He was nervous working around white people, especially white girls. He was caught off guard when one of the white waitresses came in late to work one day and hurriedly asked Richard to tie her apron. Richard soon relaxed in his new role and even learned to joke with the women. He sat around with them during breaks and listened to stories about their love lives and problems at home. He paid careful attention to everything they said, mentally taking notes for possible writing ideas.

Richard and Maggie decided that they could afford to have Ella and Leon join them in Chicago. Richard rented a two-room apartment with Maggie and sent train tickets to his mother and brother, who came to Chicago. The living arrangements were tight, with Richard providing the main income for the entire family. Aunt Maggie worked in a garment factory, but black women earned poor wages at that time.

Richard gained a temporary position at the Post Office and his financial status rose. He rented another apartment consisting of a bedroom and kitchen and moved his family, including Aunt Cleo. Richard and Leon slept in the kitchen, where the smell of food constantly kept them hungry. Cockroaches and other bugs ran rampant throughout the apartment. Richard hoped to gain full-time status at the Post Office and bring in a better salary, but because of years of malnutrition, he could not meet the 125-pound weight requirement. He was devastated.

Richard's only escapes were reading and writing. As soon as he came home from work, Richard would slump back in his bed with a book in his hand. This upset his Aunt Maggie, who scolded him for wasting his time on idle activities. Richard's mother was sick again, and this meant more money was needed to pay medical bills.

Richard disciplined himself to write each day, trying to imitate the writers he read. He took in every sentence and every paragraph, trying to decipher what made a good writer. He tried desperately to imitate their sentence structure and writing style. He wrote sentences over and over on scrap sheets of paper. "I always somehow failed to get onto the page what I thought and felt," Richard said. His family members either scoffed at or ignored his writing. They did not know what to think.

In 1929, Richard finally met the weight requirement at the Post Office and landed a full-time job working late at night. His income increased greatly—by his standards—and he once again moved his family, this time into a four-room apartment. Richard was proud of his job and the fact that he could provide for his family, especially his mother.

Richard was on his way to work on October 24 when he stopped at a newsstand. Headlines exploded with news of a stock market crash. Richard thought little of the situation. He believed blacks had nothing to lose—only white people were wealthy and therefore only white people would experience financial trouble. He could not have been more wrong. Thousands of people—black and white—lost their jobs. Richard lost his job at the Post Office.

During this time, Richard published his first professional piece, a short story entitled "Superstition." The story closely resembled the work of Edgar Allan Poe. Richard submitted a copy of the story to *Abbott's Monthly*, a black magazine. When Richard received an acceptance letter, he became excited at the possibility of being able to write short pieces for a living. The magazine promised to run the story and to pay him fifty dollars. "Superstition" appeared in the April 1931 issue of *Abbott's Monthly*, but Richard's check never arrived.

A distant cousin hired Richard to sell burial plots and life insurance policies to African Americans in Chicago's South Side. Richard visited many residences every day. He soon learned that in this business he was supposed to swindle customers into paying the insurance costs. This new job offered Richard a unique and personal view of the lifestyles and personalities of hundreds of African-American families. Richard relished this opportunity, as he was still trying to understand the minds of black people. Even in the North, most African Americans lived in poverty. He saw one tenement house after another with holes in the ceilings, fallen-in staircases, and patched windows and doors. "I was in and out of many Negro homes each day and I knew that the Negroes were lost, ignorant, sick in mind and body," Richard said. Because of the poor state of the economy, Richard was not able to keep his insurance job.

With no income and five people to support, Richard had to find a cheaper place to live. He sold a few personal belongings and rented a few rooms in a condemned building. Ella cried upon seeing the place, but Richard had no choice.

The stock market crash led to the Great Depression, which swept across the United States in the 1930s. Richard spent much of his days out on the streets, listening, watching, and thinking. With ample free time, he completed his first novel. He wrote about a Southern black woman who worked as a schoolteacher and had four children. He based his character, named Myrtle Boldon, on his own mother. Richard relished the fact that he had written a full-length novel. However, out of anger, Richard destroyed his book in a fire one day when he could find no food in the house. Desperate to eat, he paid a visit to the welfare office to beg for bread.

Richard was accustomed to not having food, but he could not stand to see his mother go hungry. While he waited for his paperwork to clear at the welfare office, he had a fascinating revelation. He looked around at the number of poor black people that had gathered for food at the relief station. As they waited together, they discussed the difficulties of their lives. The more Richard listened, the more he learned. As he sat and watched, he understood that hunger and poverty had brought these people here—not personal failure. For the first time, Richard realized that he was not alone—he was not a failure. "Their talking was enabling them to sense the collectivity of their lives, and some of their fear was passing," he said.

Richard concluded that fear was the single greatest element that held African Americans back. Fear was so ingrained in them that they had become numb to it. They reacted to it but did not know how to get rid of it. Richard wanted African Americans to unite and redefine their lives. If they could do that, "no power on earth could alter it."

During the Great Depression, Richard went through a new range of menial jobs—street cleaner, ditch digger, hospital janitor, and occasionally a postal clerk. He sent pieces of his writing to different publishers, but no one accepted his work. While he walked the streets of Chicago during the day, Richard often stopped in the park to listen to different people speak about political and racial matters. He observed black people who supported a return to their African roots. Richard enjoyed listening to their passionate speeches about black pride.

Richard also took notice of a group of Communist speakers. He did not especially care for how they communicated with the public, but he did like the fact that they promoted action. He also did not believe that the Communists truly accepted black people, although they claimed to.

In 1933, Richard got a job as a hospital janitor and began to meet at night with a few of his white coworkers. They met in one man's apartment and cooked dinner, drank, and talked. Richard learned that some of them were Communists, including one of his closest friends, Abe Aaron. Richard liked Aaron, who also wanted to be a writer. Aaron told Richard about the John Reed Club, a Communist organization for artists and writers. The club was named after John Reed, an American journalist who visited Russia in 1917 and wrote a book about the Bolshevik Revolution entitled *Ten Days that Shook the World*. Upon his return to America, Reed helped create the United States Communist Party in 1919.

When he first heard about the club, Richard told his friends that he wanted nothing to do with it. From what Richard had seen of the Communist demonstrations on the street, he was not impressed with the party. "I don't want to be organized," he told his friends. When someone suggested that the John Reed Club might help Richard to write, he said, "Nobody can tell me how or what to write."

Still, Richard craved intellectual camaraderie. He

did not have anyone with whom to discuss literature or to share his writing. One night Richard was bored and decided to go downtown and visit the John Reed Club "in the capacity of an amused spectator." He knocked on the door and a man casually welcomed him inside. Richard introduced himself and said that he liked to write. The man took Richard into another room and handed him an armload of magazines, including *New Masses* and *International Literature*. Richard had never heard of these magazines, but they had published well-known and respected writers, such as the novelist Sherwood Anderson and the poet Carl Sandburg.

Richard sat in on a meeting. For the next few hours he listened to young men and women confidently talk about what they wanted to do with their lives. He was surprised to find a group of stimulating young artists who seemed to share many of his same sentiments. He later wrote, "I was meeting men and women whom I would know for decades to come, who were to form the first sustained relationships in my life."

Richard's experience at the John Reed Club, sponsored by the Communist Party, made him a little more curious. He was not attracted to the politics of the Communist Party, but he did agree with its philosophy of organizing workers. After seeing and experiencing first-hand the poverty that black people suffered, Richard knew that something had to be done. He learned through the Communist magazines about the problems of the working class. He realized that he shared many similar concerns with these people. The Communist

Party gained strength during the Great Depression because so many people were jobless and it fought for workers' rights, unemployment insurance, and social security (before these were federal policies). These aspects caught Richard's eye. Could Communism really bring people together, despite race and social status? "The problem of human unity was more important than bread, more important than physical living itself . . . without a common bond uniting men, without a continuous current of shared thought and feeling . . . there could be no living worthy of being called human."

Maybe African Americans had found a voice through the Communist Party. He read the magazines and noticed that he shared some of the same characteristics as many of the writers, such as the poet Langston Hughes, who were poor and had dealt with discrimination. He also noticed that many of the white writers tackled the issue of race. The ideals of the party and the articles and stories in the magazines stirred him to write a poem that night. The poem was rough, but Richard felt it "linked white life with black, merged two streams of common experience." He called it "I Have Seen Black Hands," and it appeared in the June 1934 issue of *New Masses*. His angry poem ends with the hope of revolutionary revolt:

> I am black and have seen black hands
> Raised in fists of revolt, side by side with the white
>   fists of white workers,
> And some day—and it is only this which sustains
>   me—

Some day there shall be millions and millions of
  them,
On some red day in a burst of fists on a new horizon!

This poem spoke to Communists because it not only concerns racial unity, but also people rallying against capitalism in the United States.

Richard's mother noticed that he had begun to stay up late at night. She asked if he were sick. He told her that he was reading and showed her the magazines he had received at the John Reed Club. His "mother's face showed disgust and moral loathing." The crude political cartoons and Communist images on the magazines bothered her. "That picture's enough to drive a body crazy," she told him. She was skeptical of the John Reed Club and of Communism.

Richard's interest in the Communist Party decreased after he spoke with his mother. He wished he could have explained the contents of the magazines in a way that she would understand. He reread the magazines and decided that the writers and the artists had the right ideas but not the proper language. He saw this as an opportunity. "Here, then, was something that I could do." The Communists tried to deliver their message with abstract concepts, but they needed to be more concrete. They needed to better connect with their audience. Richard had a mission. "I would tell Communists how common people felt, and I would tell common people of the self-sacrifice of Communists who strove for unity among them."

During the next few months, Richard attended the John Reed Club meetings regularly. He read poems at meetings and impressed members with his writing skills. Communist publications, such as *Left Front*, *Anvil*, and *New Masses,* began publishing his poems. Richard wrote angry poems that illustrated his feelings about racism and society. He also wrote pieces that talked of the working class overpowering wealthy business owners. He began to feel at ease with the John Reed Club.

Richard had not officially joined the Communist Party, but in September 1933, the club asked him to edit their magazine, *Left Front*. Richard accepted this offer, but he soon discovered that even here black people were treated differently than white people. Nevertheless, he still hoped that the Communist Party might one day help African Americans to come together and demand justice and fair wages for their labor. He wanted to work as hard as possible and to focus his creative energies toward keeping the highest ideals of the John Reed Club alive.

Chapter Four

Exploring the Communist Party

Richard felt as though he had found a home with the John Reed Club. He gave lectures about black literature and poetry and read books by authors recommended by fellow club members, including Ernest Hemingway and James Joyce. Many visitors attended the meetings to talk about politics and social issues, such as the rise of fascism in Europe. Richard recruited young revolutionary writers to join the club. He hoped that their writing, as well as his own, would inspire a whole new generation of Americans to ignore class and race and join together to form a new ruling party of the people. The Indianapolis John Reed Club invited him to two of their meetings to speak about the poetry of Langston Hughes. He had finally found the intellectual outlet he had been seeking for so long.

Richard had managed to avoid becoming a member of the Communist Party up to this point, but in 1934, the John Reed Club elected him to serve as executive secretary. This meant that he would essentially become the club leader, and that he also had to officially join the Communist Party. Richard protested that he was too new to the group to serve as its leader, but members of the club chose him anyway. Richard soon learned that his election stemmed from internal political rivalry between the Communist and non-Communist members in the club. Non-Communists had voted for Richard because they wanted to minimize Communist power within the group. Communists, on the other hand, believed they could use Richard to achieve more power. Richard did not want to take sides. "Trying to please everybody, I pleased nobody," he said. This type of bickering was exactly the reason he had chosen *not* to become a Communist. Now he had no choice.

Richard's leadership role within the John Reed Club allowed him an inside view into the complicated world of Chicago Communism. He learned that other Communists kept watch over him because he read what they considered to be bourgeois—middle class—literature. Members of the party often stopped him and questioned him about certain books he read. "An invisible wall was building slowly between me and the people with whom I had cast my lot," Richard said. "I had to win the confidence of people who had been misled so often that they were afraid of anybody who differed from themselves."

Richard realized his fears when he attended a local Communist Party branch meeting in his own neighborhood. He showed up in a suit and tie. Richard stood up to introduce himself and read from note cards. He told the group that he was a writer. He heard giggles from the audience and saw members rolling their eyes. He wondered what he had done wrong. He would soon find out that the Communist Party opposed the John Reed Club and considered its members to be "intellectuals," or educated members of society who betrayed working class ideals. Richard was quickly labeled as one of these intellectuals.

Richard tried unsuccessfully to find a good-paying job. His moved his family, Ella, Leon, and Aunt Maggie, to a tiny sweltering attic near a set of railroad tracks. It was all he could afford, and now his grandmother Maggie had moved to Chicago to live with them. Richard was the only person in the family with a job, and his salary could not cover the cost of rent and food. They moved into increasingly cheaper and smaller apartments in an attempt to ensure that everyone would eat.

Richard continued to write whenever he found the time. His mother, along with the rest of his family, scolded him for wasting his time. Ella despised the Communist Party and worried about Richard as though he were still a young boy.

Although Richard thought his mother should not worry about his connections to the party, he began to worry himself. At the Midwest Writers' Congress held by the John Reed Club in August 1934, club members voted to take the magazine *Left Front* out of print. Richard was stunned. The club's Communist members argued that the publication took party members away from their ultimate duty—political action. The party would allow club members to write for short periods, but preferred that members allot the majority of their day to party work. Richard was furious.

The very next month the Communist Party dissolved the Chicago John Reed Club entirely. Richard noticed that the party was trying to become more revolutionary and active. Communists wanted members to focus on dissolving fascism. The party proposed a national organization of established writers called the "League of American Writers," to replace the John Reed Club. It would be centered in New York. Richard disagreed with the idea and argued that it was discriminatory. He had joined the John Reed Club to share his writing with others and to meet new up-and-coming writers. Now the party was saying that these writers were not good enough. Although Richard opposed the idea of the League of American Writers, he signed up anyway. He could not be without some sort of scholarly outlet in his life, and he knew that it could also be a good way to promote his own work.

The John Reed Club was gone, but Richard managed to find another local group of writers with whom to share his work. A small group of former John Reed Club members gathered to form their own writing group. During the fall of 1934, this group of friends would gather once a week at a member's house in the North Side of Chicago and conduct a writing workshop. Richard was ecstatic. He could not believe that he, a black, uneducated man from the South, was sitting in a white man's living room, surrounded by white college graduates, reviewing poetry and literature.

Richard came up with the idea to write about some of the more interesting people he had come across in his experiences with the Communist Party. The political motives and rebellious mindsets of these people intrigued Richard. He wanted to interview African-American Communists in Chicago. He wondered why they were interested in Communism and Socialism.

Richard interviewed a man named David Poindexter, who had led many Communist demonstrations. Richard described Poindexter as a typical African-American Communist living in Chicago:

> Southern-born, he had migrated north and his life reflected the crude hopes and frustrations of the peasant in the city. Distrustful but aggressive, he was a bundle of the weaknesses and virtues of a man struggling blindly between two societies, of a man living on the margin of a culture. I felt that if I could get his story I would make known some of the difficulties inherent in the adjustment of a folk people to an urban environment.

After visiting with Poindexter several times, Richard read over his interviews and studied the patterns of Poindexter's life. He thought about the circumstances that brought Poindexter to Chicago and wondered, "What quality of will must a Negro posses to live and die with dignity in a country that denied his humanity?" He discovered one quality he admired more than any other— Poindexter's willingness to stand up for what he believed in and not submit to authority. He spoke on dangerous street corners advocating Communism.

Poindexter also stood up in meetings and argued against decisions made by the party leaders. He was developing a reputation as a troublemaker within the party, and the more time that Richard spent with Poindexter, the more suspicious the Communist Party became of his motives. Members of the party pulled Richard aside at meetings and questioned him about his business with Poindexter. They wanted to know why Richard spent so much time with him. One party member even visited Richard at home and threatened him with expulsion from the party. "Intellectuals don't fit well into the party, Wright," the man told him. Richard was astounded. He could not figure out how he had done anything wrong. "Why was it that I was a suspected man because I wanted to reveal the vast physical and spiritual ravages of Negro life . . . What was the danger in showing the kinship between the sufferings of the Negro and the sufferings of other people?"

Richard's writing abilities caught the eye of a man named Harry Haywood, a black Communist leader in the South Side. Haywood requested Richard's presence late one evening. Richard, worried that he was in trouble with the party, hesitated to visit him. "I was suspicious. Was this a political trap? They had hurled baseless accusations at me and I felt there could be no ground of trust between us." Several days later, Richard decided he would take a chance and see what Haywood wanted. As it turned out, Haywood knew of Richard's talent and wanted him to work more directly with the party. He asked Richard to organize a committee against the high cost of living for blacks in Chicago. Richard did not like Haywood because of his sly nature, and he declined the offer, citing that he wanted to dedicate his time to writing. Haywood turned to Richard and told him, "The party has decided that you are to accept this task." Richard knew what this meant. He had no choice but to accept Haywood's offer.

Richard knew that the job would take him away from his writing. He spent his evenings talking with party members about the cost of living and the price of groceries. Richard loathed every minute of it and yearned to be at home writing.

Shortly after Richard took on the task of organizing African Americans in Chicago, Haywood asked him to represent the party at a youth conference in Switzerland and then another in the Soviet Union. Richard had always wanted to travel around the world. However, he did not want to represent the Communist Party to the rest of the world. He debated the decision over and over, but he chose not to go. He was committed to his writing and his writing workshop. He had to maintain focus on his work in order to improve. The party was not pleased with Richard's decision.

Early in 1935, Richard completed his second novel, *Lawd Today!*, about a postal worker named Jake Jackson, a violent black man from Chicago, whose cruel environment destroys all his hopes and dreams. The book was revolutionary compared to what other African Americans were writing. During this time, most black writers were a part of the movement known as the "Harlem Renaissance." Their writing style reflected pastoral imagery in a smooth manner that embraced African-American culture. *Lawd Today!* was the exact opposite. Richard wrote in an angry and pessimistic tone with no heroic characters and heavy use of satire. Richard sent the novel to many different publishers, but no one accepted it. It made them uneasy. Editors also told Richard that although he wrote short stories well, his novel had no plot. Richard revised the novel several times, but still no one wanted it. It would not be published until 1963, after Richard's death.

In April 1935, Richard and a few friends hitchhiked to New York to attend the first American Writers' Congress. The Communist Party sponsored the meeting for the League of American Writers, the group the party had formed to replace the John Reed Club. When Richard arrived, he was surprised to find that no one would give him a place to sleep. One hotel after another turned him away. Richard inquired throughout the city and finally ended up with a bed in the Harlem YMCA. He spent nine days in New York going to writers' meetings and visiting the theatre. Richard proposed a vote to keep the John Reed Club in action, but no one else took his side. He returned to Chicago feeling more discouraged about the Communist Party.

The following month, President Franklin D. Roosevelt

established the Works Progress Administration (WPA) in response to the poor economy. The WPA functioned as a work relief program to provide unemployed and underemployed people with jobs. The Federal Arts Project, a program created within the WPA, quickly caught Richard's attention. It gave jobs to writers, actors, journalists, teachers, and musicians. Richard joined the Illinois branch of the Federal Writers' Project as quickly as he could. He learned that candidates needed published pieces to be considered for a job. He submitted his two published short stories and thirteen poems and was given a job as a supervisor, an admirable position for a poor black man.

Richard earned $125 a month in his new job—a sizable increase from his previous wage of fifty dollars a month. Many of his friends from the John Reed Club had taken jobs with the Illinois Writers' Project as well. Richard, however, was the only one to become a supervisor, and he was the only black supervisor. With his impressive salary and new position, Richard moved his family into a larger apartment on Indiana Street. His new freedom allowed him to write whatever interested him.

He wrote an article about professional boxers Joe Louis and Max Baer. The men were scheduled to fight in Chicago on September 24. Joe Louis was the great grandson of a slave. A strong and skillful boxer, Joe became a hero to both white and black people and was the second African American to win the heavyweight title. Richard listened to the radio as Joe Louis beat Max Baer, a white man and former heavyweight champ.

After the fight, Richard watched and listened to black people celebrating the victory. An estimated twenty-five thousand people danced in the streets that night.

At home that night, Richard wrote effortlessly, his feelings naturally forming into words and sentences. He wrote about the psychological effects the fight had on the African-American community. In one section Richard wrote, "Here's a fleeting glimpse of the heart of the Negro, the heart that beats and suffers and hopes—for freedom." His article appeared in *New Masses*. Both white and black readers enjoyed Richard's article, and it brought positive attention from the Communist Party.

By this time, Richard had finished his interviews with David Poindexter, despite Communist warnings to drop his project. He compiled the details of Poindexter's life and some of his own childhood experiences to create a short story about a lynching called "Big Boy Leaves Home." Richard submitted the story to a writing anthology entitled *The New Caravan* in January 1936 and soon received an acceptance letter and a check for fifty dollars. The anthology was published in November. Richard was happy to have a story published by a non-Communist, white publication. It meant that his piece had been chosen because it was well written. Critics from well-known publications, such as the *New York Times,* the *Saturday Review of Literature,* and the *New Republic*, read Richard's story and praised him as a rising young talent. He finally felt like a true writer.

"Big Boy Leaves Home" marked a new literary development. Once again, the natural and realistic tone of

Poet Langston Hughes sought Richard's friendship after reading his work.
(Courtesy of the Library of Congress.)

the story departed from the typical Harlem Renaissance style. Richard wrote the dialogue of his characters in a thick, Southern dialect that black authors before him had avoided. Black authors also had avoided portraying brutality in realistic detail, but Richard painted a clear picture of the treatment of black people. His story described the tar-and-feathering and burning of an African-American youth in the South. Although these practices were common in the South, people in both the South and the North were not accustomed to reading such details in short stories.

The publication of "Big Boy Leaves Home" brought Richard unwanted attention from the Communist Party. Party officials held different opinions about Richard's newfound fame. They became increasingly suspicious of him. In Communist circles, Richard was known as the "bastard intellectual," because he thought too independently. The party wanted people to think alike. Communist leaders wanted to control what members said and wrote, including Richard. Richard fluctuated between wanting to be a good Communist and wanting to choose his own style of writing and topics to write about. He enjoyed spending time with a group that accepted all people as equals, but he valued his writing even more. Authority figures had controlled him all of his life, and he did not want his writing to be suppressed by the Communist Party.

With the success of Richard's published works, his name became known among other African-American writers of the time. Langston Hughes had read "I Have

Seen Black Hands" in *New Masses* in 1934, and he decided then that he wanted to meet Richard. Hughes visited Chicago in 1936 and looked up Richard's number in the phone book. Having no success, he attended a South Side party in hopes of spotting Richard there. Hughes was in luck—Richard was in attendance. He and Richard immediately became friends and discussed politics, writing, and traveling. Although he was not a Communist, Hughes had published some of his work in Communist publications. Hughes's first meeting with Richard established a long friendship between the two writers. From that point on, anytime Hughes came to Chicago, he always paid Richard a visit.

Around this time, Richard became involved with the South Side Writers' Group, a collection of writers who met to discuss their work. One of Richard's closest friends in the group was Margaret Walker, a young black woman from the South. A preacher's daughter, she had been raised in New Orleans. Margaret held Richard in the highest esteem as a writer. Although he was the least educated member of the group, to Margaret he was by far the most passionate and thrilling.

She quickly developed a crush on Richard, but he preferred white, rebellious women from the North with artistic backgrounds. Margaret reminded him too much of the women he had known in the South. His romantic interests, as well as other personal rivalries within the South Side Writers' Group, created friction, and the group disbanded early in 1937. Richard began looking for a new outlet.

Chapter Five

First Book

As Richard turned twenty-nine, the Communist Party in Chicago had completely turned against him. They distrusted Richard because he insisted on thinking for himself and wanted to spend his time writing and not working for the party. Richard thought about leaving the party. He still wanted to be a part of certain party programs, but he no longer wanted anything to do with the party itself.

Richard also felt that he had outgrown Chicago. He sat in his apartment one evening listening to the clacking noises of a trolley and knew that it was filled with black men and women returning home late at night to the segregated section of Chicago where most African Americans lived. He knew that the majority of the people on the trolley would be exhausted from a hard day of working for white people.

He listened to the voice of a white man on the radio, warning of a vast war developing in Europe and Asia that might affect many countries, including the United States. Richard realized that both black people and white people were suffering. Every household faced great problems, including a poor economy and high unemployment rates. Both black and white people were hungry, angry, and frustrated. He wondered if there were any hope for these people. "If this country can't find its way to a human path, then all of us, black as well as white, are going down the same drain," Richard said.

He sat at his desk, staring at a blank sheet of paper. He had so much to say, but the words would not come out. "My feelings stood in the way of my words," he said. Richard would wait, no matter how long it would take. He wanted to find the right words to describe his experiences and frustration, and then be able to make other people understand the suffering that they themselves experienced. First, he had to understand his own suffering. He had to be able to define it, to find the right kind of story that would convey his feelings. Richard's task seemed difficult, as no African-American writers had ever expressed themselves as honestly and vividly as Richard wanted to. Without the John Reed Club and his writing groups, Richard had no one to look to, no one to teach him. He decided to leave Chicago and seek a new life in New York City.

Although Richard was excited about moving to a new city, it was hard for him to leave his family behind. His mother had grown accustomed to Chicago, and the move to New York would have been difficult for her. Richard's brother had found a job and could help support his mother and aunt. His grandmother Maggie had died the previous year. Richard promised to send part of his paycheck back to his family in Chicago to take care of his mother's medical bills. In May of 1937, Richard packed his bags, including his typewriter, and hitched a ride to New York City.

Richard was not a complete stranger to New York. Two years earlier he had traveled to the city to attend the first American Writers' Congress. The second congress took place in June, just after Richard's arrival in New York. He attended the conference and heard noted speakers, including Ernest Hemingway.

The conference had a rushed feel to each session. A war between fascists and socialists and communists was beginning in Spain, and the fascists were winning. Many at the conference were convinced a world war was on the horizon and feared that fascism was on the rise. Richard was careful not to voice any opinion in opposition. Although he had wanted to sever his party ties in Chicago, he needed the party in New York. He was in a new town and needed a job as well as connections to other writers.

Although the Communist Party had been concerned about Richard's independence, they were impressed with his literary talent. The *Daily Worker*, a Communist newspaper, offered Richard a job in the paper's Harlem office. Unable to transfer his position with the Federal Writers' Project because he had not resided long enough in New York, he desperately needed work. The pay at the newspaper was low, but Richard accepted the job because it gave him the opportunity to have his work published. The *Daily Worker* was the only white newspaper to feature black writers and issues.

Richard grew to like the New York branch of the Communist Party. He saw that they actually wanted to work for the benefit of the common man—black and white. He noted that at party meetings, members did not differentiate between blacks and whites, men and women, or the educated and non-educated. Everyone was equal. The New York party was nothing like the Chicago party, and Richard found his place quickly.

Working as a reporter for the *Daily Worker*, Richard's assignments included exposing the horrible conditions of the poor black neighborhoods in New York. He focused on Harlem, where housing was appalling, rent was terribly high, and tuberculosis ran rampant. Although Harlem was mainly a black area of town, most of the businesses were owned and run by white people. Blacks and Communists protested this, and riots often ensued, along with police brutality. Richard stood in the middle of everything and watched it all take place. He wrote forty articles that he actually signed his name to, along with many anonymous articles that also ran in the *Daily Worker*.

Richard enjoyed being able to portray black issues to the rest of the country, but he was not thrilled about having to write about it in a Communist publication. He did not want to promote party propaganda or to be considered only as a Communist writer. He wanted to find a different job.

Richard began to spend time with his new friend Ralph Ellison, a writer he had met through Langston Hughes just after arriving in New York. Ellison came to visit Richard often at the paper, and the two spent hours talking about each other's stories and ideas. Both men grew up in the South, and although Ellison was the better educated of the two, he considered Richard to be one of the most fascinating and confident men he had ever met. Ellison would later publish the novel *Invisible Man*.

Richard encouraged Ellison to write a book review for the first issue of a quarterly black magazine called *New Challenge*. The magazine focused on the literature and lives of African Americans. Richard's first assignment was to write an essay about the history of Negro literature, with a focus on writing that tended to be revolutionary. Richard liked the idea and proceeded to write "Blueprint for Negro Writing," which appeared in the autumn 1937 issue of *New Challenge*.

In this essay, Richard outlined what he thought was wrong with some of the previous works of African-American authors. He proposed that most black writers, especially those of the Harlem Renaissance, had been afraid of offending their mostly white audiences. Richard's essay declared that black writers should stop trying to mimic white writers and start writing for their own black audiences. He suggested that African Americans dig down into their own experiences and write about their lives as they lived them—not as white people saw them. He wanted black writers to join together and

Richard became life-long friends with fellow writer Ralph Ellison.
(Courtesy of the Library of Congress.)

form writing groups and share their work with one another.

The essay caused a great deal of controversy. Older, more established writers, such as Zora Neale Hurston, complained that Richard's suggestions would reduce the stories of black people's lives to only those moments of intense pain caused by the crimes committed against them. Richard had just written a review of Hurston's *Their Eyes were Watching God* in *New Masses* and criticized the book for falling under the category of writing he had opposed in "Blueprint for Negro Writing." This fueled a long running argument between the two writers.

This controversial essay marked a pivotal point in the development of African-American literature. No other writers had advocated taking such a raw style when writing about black history and culture.

Richard had been excited about working for a magazine devoted entirely to African-American issues. However, he and the publisher—an old friend from Chicago—did not agree on many points. After the first issue, due to leadership problems and disagreements with many supporters, the publisher did not continue the magazine.

Richard was having the same bad luck with other publishers. He repeatedly sent out his early novels, including *Lawd Today!*, but no publisher would accept them. They each said that his writing was too bold, and his story lines were too thin for novels. Richard thought that the real reason was because the black figures in his

Richard offended established black authors of the Harlem Renaissance, such as Zora Neale Hurston, when he complained that they catered their writing to white audiences. *(Courtesy of the Yale Collection of American Literature, Beinecke Rare Book and Manuscript Library.)*

stories were not victims. He tried to use literary agents to promote his books to publishers, but discovered that agents were less willing to promote his books than the publishers were. They told him his writing was too experimental and negative. Rather than changing his style to suit the needs of publishers, Richard continued on in his angry and innovative writing style. He refused to change for anyone, because the detrimental life and harsh cruelties of blacks were what Richard intended to show to the world—one way or another.

In the summer of 1937, *Story* magazine held a writing contest open to anyone who had ever worked for the Federal Writers' Project. They offered five hundred dollars for the first place prize. The winner would also have their manuscript published in the magazine. Richard sent in a collection of short stories he titled *Uncle Tom's Children*.

He had recently received praise from reviewers at Viking Press when he submitted his essay "The Ethics of Living Jim Crow" for a WPA anthology entitled *American Stuff*. Richard waited almost half a year before he heard anything back from the judges at *Story* magazine. Then on December 15, he received a letter from the organizer of the contest. He had won! He would receive five hundred dollars in cash, and Harper & Brothers would publish *Uncle Tom's Children* in March the following year. Richard was ecstatic.

When it was published in the spring of 1938, *Uncle Tom's Children* was reviewed widely. Many critics found *Uncle Tom's Children* to be an example of fresh and powerful writing. They claimed it was the most vivid depiction of Southern black life ever written. The president's wife, Eleanor Roosevelt, publicly declared how well written the story was. Even white Southerners confessed that Richard's story was accurate in describing the horror of the Jim Crow South. Other reviewers were less positive. Zora Neale Hurston thought it was filled with nothing but hatred and violence, though she still admitted that the writing was impressive.

Early in 1938, Richard met two people in the literary business that would be of use to him in the future. Edward Aswell worked for Harper & Brothers, the company that published *Uncle Tom's Children*. Richard met Aswell one day soon after his manuscript was chosen for *Story* magazine. He was initially wary around Aswell, a middle-aged man from Memphis, Tennessee. When Aswell, an easy-going man, complimented Richard on his writing accomplishments, Richard was astonished. He had made an important contact he would keep for years to come.

Richard also met a man named Paul Reynolds Jr., who wanted to have Richard as a client. Reynolds worked for the Paul R. Reynolds literary agency, the oldest literary agency in the country. Richard had previously had no luck with literary agents, but one of his friends in the Communist Party gave his name to Reynolds. Although Reynolds was politically conservative, Richard liked him because he took his clients seriously. He spent a great deal of time looking over their manuscripts and making honest comments. Richard would work with Reynolds throughout his writing career.

In the meantime, Richard was working for the New York branch of the Federal Writers' Project. He was contributing to a book about Harlem for the WPA, as well as a book for the Writers' Project about blacks in New York. Richard was happy to be separated from party politics for a while, but trouble was brewing for the New York Writers' Project.

U.S. Congressman Martin Dies, a democrat and passionate anti-communist from Texas, took an interest in the Writers' Project's work. He and other congressmen were suspicious of the Federal Writers' Project. Dies did not like the fact that many of the writers were American communists and claimed that the Communist Party used the project as a way for young writers to voice their philosophy and eventually conspire to overthrow the U.S. government. At the time, Richard was not too concerned. He had other things to look forward to. He was making great strides as a writer, and he was not currently in conflict with the Communist Party. He had a check for five hundred dollars and finally felt like a professional writer.

Chapter Six

Reaching the Masses

In May of 1938, as *Uncle Tom's Children* was being reviewed, Richard began to think about writing a new novel. The reviews of *Uncle Tom's Children* suggested that America was ready for a realistic, even angry novel about being black in America. If he could make it good enough, develop a plot and story line over a longer narrative, he could show it to Edward Aswell at Harper & Bros. He needed a place to work with few distractions, where he could focus on his writing. He moved in with some old friends in Brooklyn, Jane and Herbert Newton. Jane and Herbert were an interracial, Communist couple Richard had known back in Chicago. The Newton's had moved to New York after a trip to the Soviet Union.

Richard was concerned about how his stories affected readers. It was possible they had an opposite effect from what he had intended. He wanted people to read his books and get angry, not tearful. "I swore to myself that if I wrote another book, no one would weep over it; that it would be so hard and deep that they would have to face it without the consolation of tears." He wanted readers to feel his own anger and hoped they would be moved enough to take action to change the conditions that black people faced every day. He did not want people to feel that merely reading his books would make racial prejudice disappear. Richard wanted his new novel to be so powerful and honest that it would be an act of revolution. Previous black writers had avoided violence and rage in their works, but Richard saw a definite need for these elements in his writing.

In June 1938, he applied to the New York Writers' Project creative work program and was accepted. All he needed to do to receive his paycheck was to sign in at the project office once a week. He could spend the rest of his time working on his novel.

Richard worked every day. He often woke up very early in the morning and went to a nearby park to write. He returned to the Newtons' home around mid-morning, and he and Jane discussed what he had written. He titled his new book *Native Son*, which referred to the main character, a black man called Bigger Thomas. The idea for Bigger Thomas, Richard stated, "goes back to my childhood." He modeled Bigger Thomas not just on one person he knew, but on several different people he had known in the South. "At all times he *took* his way, right or wrong, and those who contradicted him had him to fight. And never was he happier than when he had someone cornered and at his mercy." Richard wanted Bigger to be the most enraged and violent character in all of black literature.

Bigger Thomas was not a hero, Richard declared. He is a man who takes out his anger on white people. He buys clothes on credit and never makes payments. He steals from white people because "white folks had everything and he had nothing." Richard said that white people often referred to this kind of person as a "bad nigger." This person could do whatever he wanted. He refused to obey Jim Crow laws in the South and sat anywhere he pleased on a bus, rather than taking a seat in the section marked "colored people." Sometimes this type of person would get away with his rebellious nature because white people were afraid of him. However, these men would usually end up "shot, hanged, maimed, lynched, and generally hounded until they were either dead or their spirits broken." Richard's main point, however, was not simply to illustrate the rage of the black man, but rather the fact that people such as Bigger were a product of their societies. Bigger was not an intentionally angry man—he was a creation of American society.

Even though Richard had a clear idea of the main character in his novel, he struggled to write the story. Fear blocked his ability to express his thoughts on paper. "I felt a mental censor—product of the fears which a Negro feels from living in America—standing over me, draped in white, warning me not to write." He wondered what white people would think about Bigger Thomas. Would people say that Bigger Thomas is exactly like all black people, "sullen, angry, ignorant, emotionally unstable, depressed . . ." Richard worried what the Communist Party would think, because they wanted African Americans to appear as astounding heroes. Bigger Thomas would not fit that mold. Most importantly, Richard wondered how people of his own race would react to Bigger Thomas. Would they be ashamed of this character and what he stood for? The African-American community might reject the book because they did not want white people to know that this type of person existed. "Never did they want people, especially *white* people to think that their lives were so much touched by anything so dark and brutal as Bigger."

Bigger Thomas lives in the South Side of Chicago in a one-room apartment with three members of his family. He finds a job as a chauffeur for a rich family and eventually befriends his employer's daughter, Mary Dalton. One night he drives Mary around town with her Communist boyfriend. She has too much to drink and Bigger has to carry her to her bedroom when they get home. When he is laying Mary down in her bed, Bigger kisses her. Mary's mother walks in, but she cannot see Bigger in the dark. When Mary starts mumbling, Bigger places a pillow over her face to keep her quiet and accidentally suffocates her.

As Richard was writing the story, a young man named Robert Nixon actually committed a crime similar to Bigger's in Chicago. Nixon was caught breaking into a white woman's house. In his fright, Nixon murdered the woman with a brick. Richard's friend Margaret Walker sent him newspaper clippings covering Nixon's trial.

The last chapters of *Native Son* cover Bigger's murder trial. His lawyer argues that his client should not be held responsible for his acts, but rather that society should take the blame for making Bigger feel less than human. Richard summarized the novel as "an accusation against the society of the United States and a defense of the Negro people, who still live in conditions very similar to slavery."

Jane Newton told Richard that she did not like the last part of the book. She thought the trial was too detailed and opinionated. Richard argued that this was the only time in the book where he could bluntly express his opinions. Jane argued about other points in the novel, such as character names and motives, but Richard always followed his own instincts.

Richard worked nonstop over the summer of 1938. He completed a first draft of *Native Son* in October and sent it to Ed Aswell, who thought it needed another draft and—though he did not like the title of the book—sent Richard a contract and offered an advance of $250.

Richard wrote to his agent, Paul Reynolds, to tell him the good news. He also asked Reynolds to try to get more money for the manuscript. Reynolds informed Richard two days later that Harper & Brothers had raised his advance to four hundred dollars.

In the same month, Richard applied for a Guggenheim fellowship. His application stated that he was already working on the second draft of a novel about the crime of black youths in Chicago. Fifteen significant figures, including Eleanor Roosevelt and the director of the Federal Writers' Project, wrote recommendations for Richard.

By February 1939, Richard had completed a more polished draft of *Native Son*. He hired a young woman to type up the manuscript so that he would have a decent copy to send to his publisher. Richard was both relieved and worried. He wondered what his publisher and literary agent would have to say about the novel. Furthermore, he was still waiting in anticipation for news about the Guggenheim fellowship.

Two weeks later, after hearing positive and helpful reviews from his literary agent, Richard finally received word about the Guggenheim fellowship. Out of one thousand applicants, Richard was chosen to receive one of the sixty-nine fellowships. He would be getting twenty-five hundred dollars, which was more than twice what he made in one year with the Federal Writers' Project.

Richard sent a letter of resignation to the Writers' Project. He appreciated the project for helping him during the hard times of the Depression, but he was also worried about its future. The Dies Committee wanted to disband the project, or at least diminish its Communist influence. The leader of the project was therefore re-placed with a political conservative.

Richard continued to maintain his relationship with the Communist party while keeping his distance. The party still gave him numerous opportunities. In May that year he received an invitation to go to Moscow for a year and half and work as an editor for a Communist journal. As much as he wanted to travel, Richard knew that the job would take him away from his writing. His book *Uncle Tom's Children* had been translated into several other languages and was selling well in Europe, so that he had enough money from royalties to live fairly well. Furthermore, the political situation in Europe was growing more heated every day, and Richard did not want to be there when the war started.

After reading *Native Son*, both Ed Aswell and Paul Reynolds agreed that the courtroom scenes and newspaper articles about Bigger needed to be trimmed. Richard cut the news articles, but the courtroom speeches remained the same for the most part. He returned the revised manuscript to Aswell, who accepted it without the requested changes to the courtroom scenes. Richard could not believe how receptive Aswell had been. Most publishers were not like this. Aswell's boss did have some reservations about publishing *Native Son*, but Aswell pushed him to do it.

During this time, Richard met a young, white Jewish woman named Ellen Poplowitz, who worked as an organizer with the Communist Party in New York. Richard liked Ellen's laugh and the slight gap between her two front teeth, a feature that they shared. She was a serious young woman committed to her work. Richard could not easily grab her attention, and he found this refreshing. He had grown tired of women who liked him for superficial reasons. Richard and Ellen shared many common interests, including their love of literature.

Richard fell deeply in love with Ellen, and eventually won her affection, but he worried that she might not understand how difficult it would be to be married to a black man. Many states still barred interracial marriages. Even though people in New York seemed more liberal than most Americans, very seldom did a black man and a white woman marry. Richard and Ellen could lose their friends. Even worse was the possibility that their families might turn against them. He knew how close Ellen was to her family.

Richard proposed to Ellen at the beginning of the summer in 1939. She agreed to think about his offer while she went on vacation for the summer. Richard assumed she was actually rejecting his proposal.

At the end of the summer, Ellen called Richard and told him that she had moved out of her parents' house. She had found a place of her own and wanted Richard to meet her there. She was ready to accept his proposal. However, Richard did not want to see Ellen. During the summer he had become interested in someone else.

Dhimah Rose Meidman was a modern dancer from Russia who had a young son. Richard liked Dhimah and considered her to be an independent woman. He believed that because she was a dancer, Dhimah would understand and appreciate his own artistic abilities and would respect his need to write, just as he would respect her need to dance. They married in August 1939 in a church in Manhattan. Ralph Ellison served as best man.

In March 1940, the Book-of-the-Month Club chose

Richard married Russian-born Dhimah Meidman in 1939. *(Courtesy of the Yale Collection of American Literature, Beinecke Rare Book and Manuscript Library.)*

to run *Native Son* as its monthly selection. Both Aswell and Richard knew that this meant huge sales. Richard was the first black writer to be chosen for the club and was aware of the influence the club wielded over the country's readers. The book went to press at the first of the month, and Richard could not wait to see the outcome.

Contrary to Richard's fears that the book would not be well-received, major newspapers, such as the *New York Post*, praised *Native Son*, predicting it would win many literary prizes. Some critics described the book as a unique psychological study, and others claimed it to be a work of philosophy. *Native Son* broke several sales records. Over two hundred thousand copies sold in the first three weeks after publication. Richard received daily fan mail, and magazines and newspapers all over the country asked him to write articles. His name had even appeared on the Wall of Fame with other writers at the New York World's Fair in 1939. Suddenly, he had become a prominent writer, and the first best-selling black writer in America.

Chapter Seven

Controversy

After the publication of *Native Son*, Richard took Dhimah to Chicago to visit his family and to celebrate his success. He used some of his money to buy a house for his mother, his Aunt Maggie, and his brother.

Richard was filled with enthusiasm about the new changes in his life. However, these changes also left him feeling exhausted. He needed to get away to some place quieter than New York and decided to go to Mexico, although he would have preferred moving to Europe. Richard moved Dhimah, her son, and her mother to a large house in Cuernavaca, Mexico.

Before he left for Mexico, Richard learned of the Communist Party's reactions to his new novel. Some members liked *Native Son*, but the party as a whole was unhappy that the book featured no positive black characters and depicted Communists as too idealistic and not active enough. They were also angry that Richard had not shown his manuscript to the party before publishing it. Richard was infuriated that the party thought it had the right to censor his work.

In Mexico, Richard heard from his publisher and other writer friends that several people in Hollywood wanted to make a film of *Native Son*. Two prominent theater producers, John Houseman and Orson Welles, were interested in turning it into a play. Richard asked Ralph Ellison to make sure the two men were reputable. Ellison convinced Richard that both Houseman and Welles were talented and respected.

Richard met with Paul Green, a Pulitzer Prize-winning dramatist, about doing a stage production of *Native Son*. Richard signed a contract with Green, and the two agreed to meet in Chapel Hill, North Carolina, to work on the script together.

Richard's long-time dream had come true—he was a successful writer. At this time, when all should have been ideal, he was not happy. He had trouble concentrating on his writing in Mexico. He needed peace and privacy to work, but he could not have it. Dhimah loved society and attention and threw party after party at their rented villa. Richard became irritated and the tension between them began to affect his writing. Dhimah refused to alter her social life, and it was soon obvious that their marriage was a mistake. Richard told Dhimah that he had to leave Mexico.

Richard took a long route back to New York. He boarded a train at the Texas border and headed to Natchez, Mississippi, where some members of his family still lived, including his father.

Richard wanted to visit the South and recapture his boyhood memories. Many of those feelings were unpleasant, and Richard's trip to Natchez was hardly bearable. Before leaving Mexico, his friends had warned him that he might have forgotten what it was like to be a black man in the South. Nevertheless, Richard had confidence that he could pretend to be a submissive and ignorant black man.

He had barely crossed the border into Texas when an immigration officer began pestering him. Richard was well dressed and carried three suitcases, prompting the officer to ask him what he did for a living. Richard replied that he was a writer, but the officer seemed not to understand the answer. The look on his face implied that he had never heard of a black person being a writer. He asked Richard if he were a preacher. Richard repeated that he was a writer. The officer made Richard open all three of his suitcases, which contained Richard's clothes, his typewriter, and books. The officer could not believe what he saw and asked Richard where he was born. When Richard told him Mississippi, the officer relaxed and smiled. He proudly announced that he had known it from the start. He could always recognize a "Southern nigger."

By the time Richard reached Natchez, he felt the invisible, oppressive walls of Southern life close in on him. Signs were posted telling black people to sit in special seats and to drink from special water fountains. The territory between whites and blacks was once again clearly defined.

Richard could not believe that after all the years he had been away, nothing had changed. He found his father and paid him a visit. Richard's own life had changed tremendously, but his father's had stayed the same. "My mind and consciousness had become so greatly and violently altered that when I tried to talk to him I realized that, though ties of blood made us kin, though I could see a shadow of my face in his face, though there was an echo of my voice in his voice, we were forever strangers, speaking a different language, living on vastly distant planes of reality." Here were the people who raised Richard, the people he had once feared, and now he saw fear in their eyes. They remained in the South in a world that still allowed black people no privilege. If they made a wrong move, said a wrong word, or looked at a white person in the wrong way, their life could be in jeopardy.

Richard did not stay in Mississippi for long. He left with refreshed memories of his youth he could use in his writing. On his way back to New York, he met with Paul Green and John Houseman in North Carolina to discuss turning his novel into a screenplay. He rode back to New York with Houseman.

Dhimah had already been back in New York for ten days. Richard visited her once to tell her that he wanted to end the marriage. They were soon divorced.

Richard reestablished himself back in New York and moved back in with the Newtons. One afternoon Ellen Poplowitz stopped by to see Jane. Richard recognized her voice from the next room and knew that he still

Richard married Ellen Poplowitz in 1941. The couple would have two children. *(Courtesy of the Yale Collection of American Literature, Beinecke Rare Book and Manuscript Library.)*

loved her. They renewed their relationship and married less than five months later on March 12, 1941.

Two weeks later, on March 24, *Native Son* opened to a large audience at the St. James Theatre in New York. It received many favorable reviews. The director, Orson Welles, had startled radio audiences with his production of H.G. Welles' *War of the Worlds* in 1939. The science fiction story was about a Martian invasion and the production had been done so realistically that many listeners thought they were listening to an actual news report. Orson Welles and his partner John Houseman had turned the tiny Mercury Theater into the most prominent theatrical group in the country. *Native Son* would be Mercury's last production because Welles had just released his masterpiece, the movie *Citizen Kane*, to great reviews, and his future was now in Hollywood.

Some African-American intellectuals feared that because of the popularity of both Richard's book and his play, white people might become afraid of black people. They might dismiss their black servants and cooks, or lash out in violence out of guilt and fear. Some white people complained about the overtones of interracial romance between Bigger Thomas and Mary, the daughter of Bigger's employer. Despite these complaints, the play stayed on Broadway for several months and moved to Harlem and New Jersey theaters before touring the rest of the country. In Baltimore, the police would not allow the theater group to post any promotional pictures depicting images of Bigger Thomas and Mary. The large black audience had to cram into the upper balconies because they were not allowed to sit downstairs with white people.

The popularity of the stage version of *Native Son* caught the eye of a Hollywood producer. He made Richard an offer to produce the book as a movie, but he wanted to make two changes: change the title and replace all the black characters with white ones. Richard turned down the offer.

Richard stuck to a rigorous schedule of writing up to eight hours a day and published *Twelve Million Black Voices: A Folk History of the Negro in the United States*

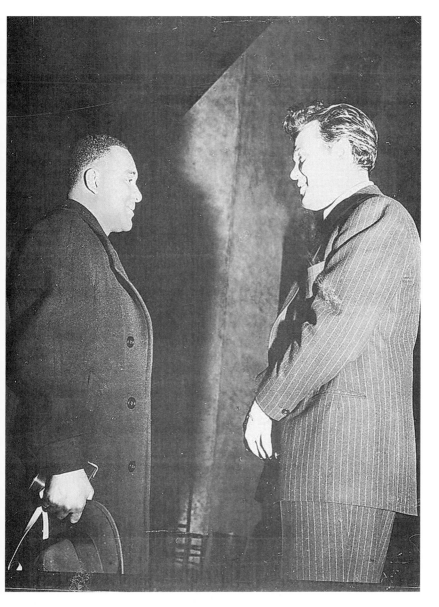

Director Orson Welles (right) created a stage version of *Native Son* that was performed on Broadway. *(Courtesy of the Yale Collection of American Literature, Beinecke Rare Book and Manuscript Library.)*

in November. It was a collection of black and white photographs, along with Richard's poetry, illustrating the lives of black people. Most white people had never seen the conditions under which black people lived; the dilapidated apartments in Harlem or the small shanties in the South. Although this book never reached the sales numbers of *Native Son*, *Twelve Million Black Voices* was a continuation of Richard's attempts to tell the story he wanted America to know—the real story of what it meant to be black in America. Ralph Ellison, who had lived in the South, cried upon reading the book.

The Japanese bombed the American naval base at Pearl Harbor on December 7, 1941, three weeks after Richard published *Twelve Million Black Voices*. President Roosevelt declared war the following day. Richard wondered what would happen to the future of the Communist Party and its different programs and publications. The House Un-American Activities Committee (HUAC) had formed in 1938. It was chaired by the nemesis of the New York Writers' Project, Congressman Dies. The committee worked closely with the Federal Bureau of Investigation (FBI) and its director, J. Edgar Hoover, to look for people they thought were engaged in unpatriotic activities. Soon after the publication of *Twelve Million Black Voices*, the HUAC wrote a formal letter to the FBI requesting that they arrest Richard and confiscate all of his books. J. Edgar Hoover sent an order to the FBI's New York office that all of Richard's work be closely reviewed for un-American ideas. They examined the photographs and the writing, looking for possible rebellious statements. The FBI had been watching Richard for some time. They were concerned about his membership in the Communist Party and feared the impact his works might have on African Americans. The FBI continued to watch Richard as he pursued his writing career, but he did not let the government stand in his way.

During this turbulent period, on April 15, 1942, Ellen gave birth to a little girl they named Julia. Richard settled into life as a husband and father. He became interested in photography and cooked lavish meals with Ellen. That same year, Richard's mother and Aunt Maggie left Chicago and moved back to Jackson, Mississippi, to live with their sister Addie.

Racial tensions increased during World War II. As the government focused on winning the war and instituted a draft, blacks were forced to serve in segregated military units and often could not work at factories where weapons were made. There was even a policy forbidding black soldiers from donating blood to army hospitals. After public protest, this policy was changed, although the blood that was donated by black people never went to white patients. The sacrifice demanded of black citizens, combined with the injustice and oppression they suffered, turned up the flame on the seething resentment that had been present for decades.

In 1943, a white police officer wounded a black soldier in Harlem, and the streets erupted in violence. Blacks fought throughout the night with police officers and members of the National Guard. Five blacks died and many others suffered injuries. Richard spoke out publicly that the riots were caused by deep-seated rage and resentment that only the poor knew. This episode deepened his commitment to reveal through his writing the true story of the lives of black people.

Chapter Eight

Black Boy

Richard's next project would be to write the story of his life. He wanted his autobiography to rid white America of the myth of the "happy," or comical Negro, a stereotype that often appeared in popular books and movies in the 1930s and 1940s. *Black Boy* describes growing up in Memphis and Mississippi and is filled with hunger, anger, frustration, and fear. Richard knew his own story was also the story of many black people, especially those who lived in the South.

In its original version, *Black Boy* covered both his Southern childhood and his experiences with the Communist Party in Chicago. The Book-of-the-Month Club selected it as a monthly selection, but only on the condition that the Chicago section be cut. Richard agreed to the change and used the Chicago section in an essay called "I Tried to be a Communist." He lashed out at their attempt to control his writing, its allegiance to the Soviet Union, and—most importantly for him—its poor treatment of black members. The essay, published in the influential *Atlantic Monthly*, was seen as a betrayal by his old comrades, who shunned him for the rest of his life.

Many people read and praised *Black Boy*, but there were still those who disapproved of the book. Theodore G. Bilbo and John Rankin, two white congressmen from Mississippi, publicly declared that the entire book was a lie. They insisted that no one in their state could have had the experiences that Richard depicted.

All the criticism did not come from racist, white Southern politicians. W.E.B. Du Bois, one of the founders of the National Association for the Advancement of Colored People (NAACP) had praised Richard's earlier works. But Du Bois was not impressed with *Black Boy*. He thought that Richard had exaggerated and had given the black characters few good qualities. Other reviewers disliked the bitter tone of the book. Overall, the book had more positive than negative reviews and added to Richard's reputation.

Aspiring writers began sending their manuscripts to Richard, asking him for advice. Richard had little time to read these manuscripts, but one young writer in particular caught his attention—James Baldwin. Baldwin grew up with many siblings and no father in a poor neighborhood in Harlem; he too wanted to write a novel about his experiences; and he disliked the black middle class. Only twenty years old, Baldwin paid Richard a visit at home in New York in May 1945. Richard welcomed Baldwin and sat for hours with the young

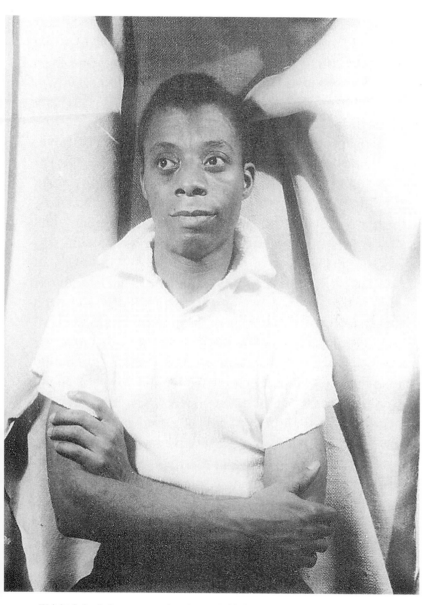

Wright helped the young author James Baldwin get his first book published. *(Courtesy of the Yale Collection of American Literature, Beinecke Rare Book and Manuscript Library.)*

man discussing his manuscript, *Go Tell it on the Mountain*. Richard encouraged Baldwin to apply for a five hundred dollar grant from Harper & Brothers and even called his friends at the publisher. In November, Baldwin learned that the Harper committee had unanimously decided in favor of giving him the money.

Richard received many invitations to travel all over the United States to lecture on race relations. He enjoyed talking to people and sharing his thoughts about how the different races could work together to ensure freedom. The lecture tour tired Richard physically and mentally. After one long series of lectures, Richard was exhausted to the point of collapse.

Richard issued a public statement officially revoking his membership in the Communist Party. Although he did not reveal his reasons in the statement, Richard said off the record that he left the party because its stance on blacks had deteriorated. He was also unhappy with the way the party had responded to *Native Son*. He wondered if his Communist friends would remain on good terms with him. He knew that the party would lash out against him, but at this point he no longer cared. He was accustomed to being in the middle of controversy, and he was glad that it had come at a time when he was enjoying the success of his new book.

Richard no longer wanted to live in New York City. Tired of the noise and hustle-bustle, he needed to find a quiet country retreat. He wanted Ellen and his daughter to live in a healthy atmosphere of fresh air and country silence. He had saved a sizable amount of money and could afford a decent house. He looked in the country and found several he liked, but no one would sell to a black man with a white wife. He finally gave up trying to find a home in the country and bought a home in Greenwich Village, a community of artists in lower Manhattan. They had found a home, but the Wrights were both growing tired of the discrimination. Even in New York, they experienced a great deal of racism. Interracial couples were still looked down upon, and sometimes they feared for their safety. Richard and Ellen wanted to escape this fear and go to a place where they could feel safe.

For years, Richard had dreamed of visiting France. He knew from other black writers, including Langston Hughes, who had lived in Paris for a short time, that Paris treated black visitors no differently than other visitors. Richard wanted to know more about the literary culture of Paris. Early in 1945, he applied for a passport. He waited anxiously for it to arrive so that he could make definite travel plans. He soon received a letter from the State Department reporting that they would not grant him a passport. A letter accompanying the passport stated that because of the turmoil created by the war, the U.S. government did not want Americans traveling to foreign countries.

Richard applied again, explaining that he had enough money to assure his family's safe welfare and return to the United States if necessary. The State Department's answer remained the same. The news infuriated Richard, who could not go to France without a passport.

Even though the government claimed that safety was the reason for not giving him a passport, Richard was convinced that it was because of his race and his former membership in the Communist Party.

Richard asked French officials to send letters to the U.S. State Department stating that he had been invited to speak in Paris. Richard called the State Department and was told that no documentation had arrived. He asked the official in France to send it again. On April 26, the French government sent Richard a formal invitation to come to Paris. Determined to get his passport, Richard flew to Washington and dealt with the State Department in person. He finally received visas for his family three days before their ship was scheduled to leave New York City.

On May 8, 1946, Richard, Ellen, and Julia stepped off their ship onto French soil. Richard's books had been translated into French, and reporters anxiously awaited his arrival. People recognized him on the street and smiled at him. Richard was so enthralled with their friendliness that he pushed himself to respond to them in French, even though he had mastered only a limited vocabulary.

In Paris, Richard developed friendships with several important writers. Many of these writers were expatriates from America, including Gertrude Stein, who was influential in literary circles in France. Stein became one of Richard's closest allies. After she read *Black Boy*, Stein began writing letters to Richard. She had once joked that she and Richard were fellow geniuses.

Unfortunately, Stein died shortly after his arrival.

Although Richard and his family felt at home in Paris, they returned to America the following January. His newfound French friends asked why he did not want to stay in France. Richard answered that he sensed something important was about to happen in America, something that would dramatically affect African Americans.

Richard arrived back in America in February 1947, hoping to find positive changes in his home country. Instead, he came back to a place that was about to become a nightmare for him. With the collapse of the U.S.-Soviet alliance following the defeat of Germany, and the beginning of the tension between the two super powers that would result in the Cold War, the fear of Communism became a driving force in American politics. The FBI and other government agencies stepped up their investigations of American Communists and spied on anyone affiliated with Communism.

Not long after his return, Richard remembered why he had left America in the first place. He had to travel from Greenwich Village to Harlem to get a haircut because no barber in Greenwich Village would cut a black person's hair. He could only eat at certain restaurants without having salt poured into his coffee, a typical prank towards black people. He and Ellen often endured racial slurs when they walked the streets of New York. Although he had grown accustomed to these challenges, Richard did not want his daughter to suffer. He cringed when she was not allowed to use the bathroom in a department store. Richard wanted Julia to grow up without the fear and anger that he harbored. They sold their home in Greenwich Village and moved back to Paris in August 1947. He had left his native country behind.

In an interview with a French journalist, Richard explained why he could no longer live in America:

> My country . . . shows concern for all the world. It is one of the most beautiful traits of our national character. One is concerned about the Chinese and the Armenians, and rightly so. Yet one never thinks of the destitution of blacks who are right here, outside the door, on the sill. One is concerned with free elections in Greece, but Mr. Byrnes, our Secretary of State . . . is opposed to abolishing the poll tax, which prevents almost all blacks in the Southern states from voting.

Richard quickly settled into his new life in France. In January 1949, Ellen gave birth to a girl they named Rachel. Richard gained a comfortable distance from his troubles in the United States. He opened his mind to more global issues and his writing took on a more international tone as he focused on social issues in countries in Africa, the Middle East, and Asia. He continued to mull over the racial conditions that existed in America, but he also began to look at injustices imposed on people all over the world.

Richard became involved in the anti-colonial movement. Several European countries had colonized Africa in order to have access to its natural resources. The continent suffered deeply from this European domination and members of the international Pan-African movement opposed colonization.

Richard helped his French-speaking African friends create a new journal called *Présence Africaine*. A friend from Senegal was editor, and Richard served on the editorial board, along with other men from Senegal. Jean-Peal Sartre and Albert Camus, two famous French philosophers and writers, became patrons of the journal. This Pan-African group wanted to make African culture well known in Europe. Richard advocated *Présence Africaine* to black American readers. American authors and poets, such as Gwendolyn Brooks from Chicago, published their work in the journal.

Richard's books had been translated into several foreign languages and the play *Native Son* was performed on several European stages, giving Richard a worldwide audience. He traveled extensively to give lectures. No matter where Richard went, he related to the suffering of local people. He searched for a way to promote human dignity, seeking, as he always had, a way for people to gain their civil rights.

Chapter Nine

Expatriate

Richard was finally able to relax while living in Europe. This new atmosphere helped his productivity. He wrote more novels, collections of essays, and many poems. He worked with George Plimpton to create the internationally renowned literary magazine *Paris Review* and continued to work as a journalist. Richard Wright was a respected name in literary circles. The new ease, however, came at a price. Living as an expatriate in France drained much of the anger that had fueled his best writing.

In the summer of 1949, Pierre Chenal, a French film director, approached Richard about making *Native Son* into a film. Richard had turned down American filmmakers before, but he respected Chenal and agreed to write the screenplay. The filmmakers thought that Richard would be a perfect Bigger Thomas. Richard laughed and said he would have to take acting lessons first, but Chenal said that he simply needed to lose weight to look the part. Richard agreed to play the role, although he was forty years old, and the character of Bigger Thomas was supposed to be a nineteen-year-old teenager. Once the movie went into production, the majority of filming took place in Buenos Aires, Argentina, far away from Hollywood.

Richard loved movies and was thrilled with the idea of seeing his own work on the screen. "To make the screen version of a novel into which I had put so much of myself . . . was a dream which I had long hugged to my heart, and it was quite painful until it happened," Richard told an interviewer. To play the role of the main character, Richard had to lose a great deal of weight. He exercised often with a punching bag and rowing machine and managed to drop his weight down from 170 to 145 pounds.

African-American movie characters were usually depicted according to popular stereotype. Black actors usually played perpetually frightened characters who were always the butt of a joke. There were no such black characters in *Native Son*.

Many people in Richard's movie had never acted before. A tourist visiting South America, a nightclub dancer, a sixteen-year-old Brazilian girl studying English, and a mechanic from New Guinea each had parts. Richard, who had no acting experience either, fit in well with the rest of the cast.

The filmmakers completed the movie in June 1950. Richard had been away from his family for over ten months. Ellen grew depressed from going so long with-

Richard played the role of Bigger Thomas in the movie-version of *Native Son.* *(Courtesy of the Yale Collection of American Literature, Beinecke Rare Book and Manuscript Library.)*

out seeing her husband. At first she received many letters from him, but as time passed, the letters became less and less frequent—and less thoughtful and loving. She worried that Richard was having an affair in Buenos Aires, and she eventually learned that he was. Ellen was devastated, but nonetheless she hoped that the affair would end soon and Richard would return home to be with his family.

Native Son turned out to be a big success in Buenos Aires. Richard felt sure of similar success in America.

However, he began to have doubts when the New York State Board of Censors insisted that the film be heavily edited before it was released. Several long scenes were cut because of their Communist overtones. When the movie premiered in New York, the film critics did not treat it kindly.

Native Son traveled around the United States and met with mixed success. People in New Jersey liked it, but censors in Pennsylvania, Wisconsin, and Ohio refused to show it. It played in Chicago, but because of recent race riots, it did not play to large audiences. The movie went to Europe next, where it did somewhat better because audiences were able to see the edited parts of the film. Also, Europeans had not previously seen *Native Son* performed on stage, which was a much better production, and had little to compare the movie to. Richard tried to obtain a copy of the original version of the film for himself, but the producers avoided his requests. Then Richard found out that the movie company had gone bankrupt. He never received a copy of the movie.

When he arrived home in Paris in 1950, Richard's marriage was in trouble. Ellen had been deeply hurt by his infidelity. Adding to her injury, Richard threatened to leave and stay with the woman he had been seeing in Argentina. Ellen desperately replied that the other woman could come to Paris and be with Richard, as long as he would live at home. Ellen told Richard that he was ruining her life, but he apparently did not care.

Richard grew lonely in Paris. He had lost the rage

that inspired his earlier work, and although he still had money, he would have to write a novel soon in order to have enough money for the future. He heard only bad news from his family back in America. His mother, at age seventy, was becoming senile and could no longer think for herself. Richard blamed his family in America and in Paris for distracting him from his work. He decided to leave Paris and go to London for a few months to see if he could concentrate better there.

Richard stayed in a tiny apartment in London from February to April in 1952. He did nothing but write. At the end of April he had completed a first draft of *The Outsider*, a novel about a young black intellectual named Cross Damon who wants to be free of all ideologies and responsibilities. The book was a forceful attack on Communism.

Richard submitted a first draft to Paul Reynolds that fall, but Reynolds returned it with the request for a great deal of revision. Richard cut out a third of the novel in order to have it published, and the end result did not please him, nor did it please his readers. Critics praised the writing itself but felt that Richard had lost touch with his characters.

Richard was still haunted by his former connections to the Communist Party. Party members around the world verbally attacked him for the way he left the party and would continue to do so for the rest of his life. On the other side, the U.S. government continued to harass him for his past membership. In 1953, a young man from the U.S. State Department showed up at

Richard's wife, Ellen, and daughters Rachel (right) and Julia (left), remained in France while he was gone for long periods of time. *(Courtesy of the Yale Collection of American Literature, Beinecke Rare Book and Manuscript Library.)*

Richard's apartment in France. He questioned Richard about his old friends in the Chicago John Reed Club. Richard refused to say a word and said that the U.S. government could not scare him with its threats. Richard secretly worried though when he learned that his books were being pulled from the shelves of European libraries.

Richard began to feel that everyone around him was attacking him in some way. The Communist party, the U.S. government, and even some of Richard's writing friends had turned against him. Even Richard's former protégé, James Baldwin, reportedly fumed that Richard had left nothing for other African Americans to write about.

Feeling lonely and abandoned, Richard decided to travel to Africa—something he had always wanted to do. He felt that Africa was part of his identity and part of the roots of all black people. He planned a trip to the Gold Coast of Africa in 1953. Before he left, Richard spent time in London with friends who were familiar with African culture. He asked about polygamy, or having more than one wife, and African mysticism.

Richard set sail for Africa on June 4 and soon became ill. He had a high fever and could barely eat. He finally felt better a few days later, just before he reached Africa. Then he stepped off the ship into the nearly unbearable heat and humidity of Africa. The poor conditions there appalled him. He saw unsanitary streets, open sewers, and invalid beggars everywhere he turned.

Richard spent weeks traveling to different parts of

Africa, giving speeches, meeting important figures, attending political meetings, and taking photographs. He was curious about every aspect of African culture and constantly asked questions. He was intrigued by the similarities the people of the continent shared with African Americans. He pondered the idea that race could be biological and not just a socially constructed myth.

Over time, though, Richard became less enthusiastic about being in Africa and lost sight of his purpose for going. He noticed that the people shied away from him, and he worried that he had offended them in some way. He tried to leave early but could not find a way out.

Richard rented a car and traveled among the bush and jungle. He wanted to see the other side of African culture. After touring the jungle for three weeks, Richard could not understand how black American writers, such as W.E.B. Du Bois, had visited Africa and written about the continent, yet had failed to mention the Africa he had seen.

Richard returned to Paris in September 1953 with a plethora of photographs and scribbled notes. He wrote about his travels in a book entitled *White Man, Listen!* Published in 1957, it was one of his last works of nonfiction. He concluded one of his essays with a comment on the influence of white people:

> What I dread is that the Western white man, confronted with an implacably militant Communism on the one hand, and with a billion and a half colored people gripped by surging tides of nationalist fanati-

cism on the other, will feel that only a vengeful unleashing of atom and hydrogen bombs can make him feel secure. I dread that there will be an attempt at burning up millions of people to make the world safe for the 'white man's' conception of existence . . . There is no doubt that atom or hydrogen bombs can destroy much of human life on this earth. If the white West should attack the body of mankind in this fashion, it will not only sacrifice its own civilization, but will set off reactions of racial and religious hatreds that will last for generations.

A *New York Times* book review called *White Man, Listen!* an indignant book. The article said that the book should be taken seriously because Richard had touched on important issues. In this book, Richard wrote a thesis of his life, compiling thoughts from his earliest experiences of racial prejudice as a child with more recent examples of oppression from all around the world.

By 1958, Richard's life took a turn for the worse. He had written several more books, but they did not receive positive reviews, and none of them sold well. His mother's health was failing, and the monthly money he sent to her had to be increased to pay for her medical bills. On January 13, 1959, Ella Wright passed away at her son Leon's house.

Later that year, Richard fell ill from amoebic dysentery, a disease he had picked up during his travels. He wanted to live permanently in London, where Ellen and their children were currently residing. To do so, he first

Richard's last acclaimed book, *White Man, Listen!*, admonished the "white West," warning that its desire to control the lives of nonwhites would result in global catastrophe. *(Courtesy of the Yale Collection of American Literature, Beinecke Rare Book and Manuscript Library.)*

had to apply for a visa. London officials issued Richard a temporary visa and assured him that upon settling in England, permanent status would be granted, but it never was. Richard had already sold his home in France. He confronted British officials but received no concrete answers for their denying him a permanent visa. He knew that the American FBI had monitored his activities since the end of World War II. Richard suspected that someone was working against him. With Ellen and the children safely established in England, Richard returned to France alone. Ellen would remain in England and promote his books. Richard would rest, regain his health, and write a new novel in Paris.

By 1960, Richard continued to battle his illnesses. Each time he felt well, he soon came down with a new sickness. His diminishing energy allowed him only short periods of writing. He tired easily and spent much time in bed. In the midst of his miseries, Richard met a Russian doctor, Vladimir Schwartzmann. Upon walking into the doctor's office for the first time, the first thing that Richard noticed was a copy of his own book, *White Man, Listen!* on the doctor's desk.

Dr. Schwartzmann put Richard on a strict diet and prescribed medication. Richard responded well to the treatment and finally believed his health would be restored. Then he began to suffer relapses. He felt strong for several days, but the pain, discomfort, chills, and fever always returned.

Richard eventually returned to his vigorous schedule of writing ten or more hours each day. He no longer wrote angry novels, short stories, or essays. Instead he wrote haikus, a Japanese form of poetry that consists of three unrhymed lines and seventeen syllables. In several poems Richard expresses humor dealing with everyday occurances in life.

Richard explained why he liked writing these short poems: "These haikus . . . were written out of my illness. I was, and am, so damnably sensitive. Never was I so sensitive as when my intestines were raw. So along came that Japanese poetry and harnessed this nervous energy," said Richard. He wrote four thousand haikus that eventually were published under the title *Haiku: This Other World* in 1998.

In late 1960, Richard became seriously ill again. He stayed in bed with a high fever. Anytime he sat up, he became dizzy and broke out in a sweat. He could not keep any food down. At eighteen years old, his daughter Julia moved back to Paris to help take care of him.

Richard entered a medical clinic in Paris on November 25 to be tested and to rest. Friends visited him and were surprised that he looked so healthy. On the third day, Richard received his test results. His organs appeared healthy, and his blood pressure and weight were normal. Richard called his wife and assured her that nothing was seriously wrong with him.

On the evening of November 28, 1960, Richard placed the book he had been reading on the table next to his hospital bed. As he reached to turn out the light, he felt a sharp pain in his chest. He pushed the button to summon his nurse. But by the time the nurse reached his hospital room, it was too late. Richard was dead.

Ellen returned to Paris to meet Julia. A small funeral took place on the morning of Saturday, December 3, 1960. Ellen and Julia attended together with a group of Richard's friends. Richard's body was placed in a coffin along with a copy of the first edition of his autobiography, *Black Boy*. The inscription on the book read, "For Ellen and Julia who live always in my heart."

Timeline

1908—Richard Wright born September 4, in Roxie, Mississippi.

1910—Brother Leon Alan born September 24.

1911—The Wrights move to Memphis, Tennessee. Nathan abandons family.

1915—Attends the Howe Institute.

1916—Moves to Arkansas to live with aunt.

1919—Richard is forced to leave school and find a job. Mother suffers paralyzing stroke.

1920—Moves to Jackson, Mississippi.

1921—Richard enters fifth grade at Jim Hill School.

1924—Attends Smith Robertson Junior High School; "The Voodoo of Hell's Half-Acre" appears in the *Southern Register.*

1925—Chosen as valedictorian of the ninth grade class at Smith Robertson Junior High; end of formal education; moves to Memphis, Tennessee.

1927—Moves to Chicago.

1929—Receives full time position at the U.S. Post Office; short story "Superstition" published in *Abbott's Monthly.*

1931—Laid off at post office and begins to sell burial and funeral insurance on Chicago's South Side.

1933—Attends John Reed Club; becomes editor of club magazine, *Left Front.*

1934—Elected secretary of John Reed Club and joins Communist Party; poem "I Have Seen Black Hands" published in *New Masses.*

1935—Completes *Lawd Today!*; attends first American Writers' Congress; works for Federal Writers' Project; writes his first journalistic piece, an article about boxer Joe Louis.

1936—"Big Boy Leaves Home" published in *The New Caravan* anthology.

1937—Moves to New York City; attends second American Writers' Congress; becomes Harlem editor of the *Daily Worker*; writes "Blueprint for Negro Writing," for *New Challenge.*

1938—*Uncle Tom's Children* published; works for the New York Writers' Project.

1939—Marries Dhimah Rose Meidman.

1940—*Native Son* published; moves to Cuernavaca, Mexico.

1941—Marries Ellen Poplowitz; *Native Son*, directed by Orson Welles, appears on a Broadway; *Twelve Million Black Voices: A Folk History of the Negro in the United States* published.

1942—Daugher Julia Wright born on April 15.

1943—FBI begins its investigation that will continue to the end of Richard's life.

1945—Publication of Richard's autobiography, *Black Boy*; officially renounces membership in Communist Party.

1947—Moves family to France.

1949—Daughter Rachel born on January 17; writes screen play and stars in film version of *Native Son.*

1952—Moves to London.

1953—*The Outsider* published; travels to Africa.

1957—*White Man, Listen!* published.

1959—Becomes ill with amoebic dysentery; moves to London.

1960—Dies of a heart attack in Paris on November 28.

Sources

CHAPTER ONE: A Troubling Beginning

p. 13, "Hunger had always been more or less at my elbow . . ." Richard Wright, *Black Boy* (Harper & Brothers Publishers, New York, 1945), 13.

p. 15, "Kill that damn thing!" Ibid., 10.

p. 15, "You owe a debt you can never pay." Ibid., 11.

p. 15, "The odor of alcohol stung my nostrils." Ibid., 18

p. 20, "villain who wanted a widow's home." Ibid., 144.

p. 21, "I know what's best for you." Ibid., 153.

p. 21, "the people are coming to hear the students . . ." Ibid., 153.

p. 21, "You're just a young, hot fool," Ibid., 154.

p. 21, "I did not care if they liked it or not," Ibid., 156.

p. 22, "faced the world." Ibid.

CHAPTER TWO: Memphis

p. 23, "The shop was always crowded with black men . . ." Wright, *Black Boy*, 157.

p. 24, "After a moment or two I heard shrill screams." Ibid.

p. 24, "Boy, that's what we do to niggers . . ." Ibid.

p. 25, "Oh, no!" Ibid., 158.

p. 25, "Ain't you learned to say *sir* to a white man yet?" Ibid., 158.

p. 30, "We two black boys, each working," Ibid., 207.

p. 30, "He's trying to make us kill each other for nothing," Ibid., 208.

p. 30, "Now, you're acting like a nigger with some sense," Ibid.

p. 31, "Our plans and promises now meant nothing . . ." Ibid., 212.

p. 31, *"Dear madam: Will you please let this nigger boy . . ."* Ibid., 216.

p. 32, "You're not using these books, are you?" Ibid., 217.

p. 32, "Yes, this man was fighting, fighting with words," Ibid., 218.

p. 32, "but how on earth anybody had the courage to say it." Ibid.

CHAPTER THREE: Finding a Voice

p. 34, "Finally, sheer wish and hope prevailed . . ." Wright, *Black Boy*, 223.

p. 37, "Working with them day to day . . ." Richard Wright, *American Hunger* (Harper & Row Publishers, New York, 1977), 10.

p. 38, "I always somehow failed to get onto the page . . ." Ibid., 22.

p. 40, "I was in and out of many Negro homes . . ." Ibid., 37.

p. 41, "Their talking was enabling them to sense. . ." Ibid., 43.

p. 41, "no power on earth could alter it." Ibid., 44.

p. 42, "I don't want to be organized," Ibid., 60.

p. 42, "Nobody can tell me how or what to write." Ibid.

p. 43, "in the capacity of an amused spectator." Ibid., 61.

p. 43, "I was meeting men and women . . ." Ibid., 62.

p. 44, "The problem of human unity . . . " Ibid., 63.

p. 44, "linked white life with black . . ." Ibid., 64.

p. 45, "mother's face showed disgust and moral loathing." Ibid., 65.

p. 45, "That picture's enough to drive a body crazy," Ibid.

p. 45, "Here, then, was something that I could do," Ibid.

p. 45, "I would tell Communists how common people felt. . ." Ibid., 66.

CHAPTER FOUR: Exploring the Communist Party

p. 48, "Trying to please everybody, I pleased nobody," Wright, *American Hunger*, 69.

p. 48, "An invisible wall was building slowly," Ibid., 78.

p. 51, "Southern-born, he had migrated north . . ." Ibid.

p. 51, "What quality of will must a Negro possess . . ." Ibid., 89.

p. 52, "Intellectuals don't fit well . . ." Ibid., 79

p. 52, "Why was it that I was a suspected man . . ." Ibid., 82.

p. 52, "I was suspicious," Ibid., 100.

p. 53, "The party has decided that you are to accept this task." Ibid., 106.

p. 56, "Here's a fleeting glimpse of the heart of the Negro." Richard Wright, "Joe Louis Uncovers Dynamite," *New Masses* (September 1935).

CHAPTER FIVE: First Book

p. 61, "If this country can't find its way to a human path," Wright, *American Hunger*, 135.

p. 61, "My feelings stood in the way . . ." Ibid.

CHAPTER SIX: Reaching the Masses

p. 71, "I swore to myself that if I wrote another book," Richard Wright, *How 'Bigger' was Born: The Story of Native Son* (New York: Harper, 1940).

p. 72, "goes back to my childhood." Ibid., 854.

p. 72, "At all times he *took* his way. . ." Ibid.

p. 73, "white folks had everything and he had nothing." Ibid., 855.

p. 73, "bad nigger." Ibid.

p. 73, "shot, hanged, maimed, lynched . . ." Ibid., 857.

p. 73, "I felt a mental censor—product of the fears . . ." Ibid., 867.

p. 73, "sullen, angry, ignorant, emotionally unstable, depressed. . . ." Ibid., 868.

p. 74, "Never did they want people, especially *white* people . . ." Ibid., 869.

p. 75, "an accusation against the society . . ." Keneth Kinnamon and Michel Fabre, *Conversations with Richard Wright* (Jackson, Miss.: University Press of Mississippi, 1993), 32.

CHAPTER SEVEN: Controversy

p. 83, "Southern nigger." Constance Webb, *Richard Wright, A Biography* (New York: G.P. Putnam & Sons, 1968), 201.

CHAPTER EIGHT: Black Boy

p. 98, "My country . . . shows concern for all the world . . ." Kinnamon and Fabre, *Conversations with Richard Wright*, 97.

CHAPTER NINE: Expatriate

p. 102, "To make the screen version of a novel . . ." Kinnamon and Fabre, *Conversations with Richard Wright*, 143.

p. 107, "What I dread is that the Western white man . . ." Richard Wright, *White Man Listen!* (New York: Harper Collins, 1995), 42–43.

p. 109, "With a twitching nose/ A dog reads a telegram/ On a wet tree-trunk" Michel Fabre, *The Unfinished Quest of Richard Wright*, Translated by Isabel Barzun (New York: William Morrow & Company, Inc., 1973), 506.

p. 109, "These haikus . . . were written out of my illness . . ." Ibid., 508.

Major Works

Uncle Tom's Children: Four Novellas. New York: Harper, 1938.

Native Son. New York: Harper, 1940.

How "Bigger" was Born: The Story of Native Son. New York: Harper, 1940.

Native Son: A Play in Ten Scenes. With Paul Green. New York: Harper, 1941.

Twelve Million Black Voices. New York: Viking Press, 1941.

Black Boy. New York: Harper, 1945.

The Outsider. New York: Harper, 1953.

White Man, Listen! New York: Doubleday, 1957.

THE FOLLOWING BOOKS WERE PUBLISHED POSTHUMOUSLY:

Lawd Today! New York: Walker, 1963.

American Hunger. New York: Harper & Row, 1977.

Haiku: This Other World. New York: Arcade, 1998.

Bibliography

Fabre, Michel. *The Unfinished Quest of Richard Wright.*
Translated by Isabel Barzun. New York: William Morrow
& Company, Inc., 1973.

Gates, Henry Louis Gates, Jr., and K.A. Appian, eds. *Richard
Wright, Critical Perspectives Past and Present.* New York:
Amistad, 1993.

Kinnamon, Keneth, and Michel Fabre. *Conversations with
Richard Wright.* Jackson: University Press of Mississippi,
1993.

Rowley, Hazel. *Richard Wright: The Life and Times.* New
York: Henry Holt and Company, 2001.

Urban, Joan. *Richard Wright: Author.* New York: Chelsea
House, 1989.

Walker, Margaret. *Richard Wright, Daemonic Genius.* New
York: Amistad, 1988.

Webb, Constance. *Richard Wright, A Biography,* New York:
G. P. Putnam & Sons, 1968.

Wright, Richard. *American Hunger.* New York: Harper &
Row, 1944, 1977.

————. *Black Boy*. New York: Harper and Brothers Publishers, 1945.

————. *Richard Wright: Early Works*. New York: Library of America, 1991.

————. *Uncle Tom's Children*. New York: HarperPerennial, 1993.

————. *White Man Listen!* New York: HarperCollins, 1995.

Websites

Richard Wright: Black Boy. A film documentary by PBS.
http://www.pbs.org/rwbb/rwtoc.html

The Mississippi Writer's Page: Richard Wright.
http://www.olemiss.edu/depts/english/ms-writers/dir/
wright_richard/

View original FBI files on Richard Wright.
http://foia.fbi.gov/rnwright.htm

Index